WHY SHE BUYS

WHY SHE BUYS

**The New Strategy for Reaching the
World's Most Powerful Consumers**

BRIDGET BRENNAN

CROWN
BUSINESS
NEW YORK

Copyright © 2009, 2011 by Bridget Brennan

All rights reserved.
Published in the United States by Crown Business,
an imprint of the Crown Publishing Group,
a division of Random House, Inc., New York.
www.crownpublishing.com

CROWN BUSINESS is a trademark and CROWN and
the Rising Sun colophon are registered trademarks
of Random House, Inc.

Female Factor$_{sm}$ is a trademark of Female Factor Corp., and
use is prohibited without advance written permission.

Originally published in hardcover in slightly different form
in the United States by Crown Business, an imprint of the
Crown Publishing Group, a division of Random House, Inc.,
New York, in 2009.

Crown Business books are available at special discounts for bulk
purchases for sales promotions or corporate use. Special editions,
including personalized covers, excerpts of existing books, or
books with corporate logos, can be created in large quantities
for special needs. For more information, contact Premium Sales at
(212) 572-2232 or e-mail specialmarkets@randomhouse.com.

Library of Congress Cataloging-in-Publication Data
is available upon request.

ISBN 978-0-307-45039-5
eISBN 978-0-307-45040-1

Printed in the United States of America

BOOK DESIGN BY BARBARA STURMAN
COVER DESIGN BY WHITNEY COOKMAN
COVER PHOTOGRAPHY BY GETTY IMAGES

10 9

First Paperback Edition

TO ERIK,

who makes me happy to be alive

CONTENTS

WHY SHE BUYS

WOMEN ARE
FEMALES FIRST
AND CONSUMERS SECOND

The salesmen were all standing at attention as my husband and I walked through the doors of the car dealership. After months of searching, we knew we'd found our dream car. We strode into the place with confidence. In a few short hours, we'd be walking out with three thousand pounds of fine German steel. The tallest salesperson stepped forward, thrust out his hand, and said he'd be happy to help us. He had a firm grip. Things were looking good.

The test drive was incredible. It was a BMW 540i, and it's not called the ultimate driving machine for nothing. But I noticed something that seemed like . . . well . . . a flaw. At first I was afraid to mention it, even to myself. Who was I to question the magnificence of Bavarian engineering? Then I closed my eyes and imagined myself commuting to work every morning, and I could no longer keep silent. I hope you won't judge me harshly, but it was . . . here goes . . . the cup holders. Yes, the cup holders.

If you've ever driven a European car, you know what I'm talking about. The cup holders in this model were almost comically inadequate—like tiny plastic crab claws that made a feeble grasping motion when you touched a button. The little claws didn't seem like they could handle a sippy cup, let alone the tall, battered coffee thermos that was my constant companion.

I sat through the rest of the test drive in silence, listening to the salesman deliver a stream of performance terms including *torque* and *zero-to-sixty,* just like in the commercials, before I got up the nerve to say something. This wasn't my first car-buying experience, and I knew the disdain with which many of these guys—and they are overwhelmingly guys—view women buyers like me. How badly would I be mocked for this? I braced myself and said the words.

"What's up with the cup holders?"

He stared at me.

"They're right here."

He moved the crab claws in and out.

"Yes, but they don't seem strong enough to hold a normal cup of coffee."

Silence.

The salesperson then shot my husband a look that could be understood in any language to mean, *You poor thing, how do you stand her?* I cringed. My husband looked sheepish. I cringed again. And then the salesman said the first of two things that ensured he would never have my business or the business of anyone who knew me.

"Europeans don't eat or drink in their cars."

While I occasionally suffer from an identity crisis, in this case I knew with 100 percent certainty that I was not, in fact, a European.

"I'm American and I do drink in the car. In fact, I drink a cup of coffee every morning on the way to work. It's a tall thermos—you know, the kind you buy at Starbucks."

And then he went for a second jab, this time below the belt.

"Well, then why don't you just stick it between your legs?"

You can guess the ending to this story. We did not purchase the dream car from this man, on principle, and found the car somewhere else a month later, after my husband discovered a website selling aftermarket cup holders specifically for the 540i. The night of the dealership incident, I went on the consumer review website Epinions.com and was overjoyed to find dozens of other people lamenting the state of the cup holders in this particular model. I felt vindicated. It appeared that the aftermarket in custom cup holders for all kinds of European cars was thriving. It wasn't just me.

These days, it's never just me. Women now dominate consumer purchasing to such a degree that some companies, like Procter & Gamble, have started simply referring to consumers with the pronoun *she*.

In the automotive industry, for example, women buy more than half of all new cars and trucks and influence 80 percent of all automotive purchases.[1] Influence means that if the woman doesn't like a car's coffee cup holders, the couple (if she has a spouse) walks out of the dealership empty-handed. Women not only have money, they have veto power. It's the most powerful one-two punch in the consumer economy.

As women all over the world continue joining the workforce—earning their own paychecks as well as driving the spending of their spouses'—they have become the alpha consumers of planet Earth. As a result, executives in almost every industry are scrambling to create products and programs with female appeal, particularly in gender-neutral and traditionally "male" product categories like electronics, insurance, automobiles, and finance.

The BMW story provides a classic example of how gender differences play out at their best—and worst—in business. Women will pay attention to aspects of a product that salespeople, particularly male ones, may consider unimportant or irrelevant, whether it's the number of electrical outlets in a new home, the style of reports submitted by a consulting firm, or the quality of cup holders in a new car. In the case of the BMW, I knew from previous experience that spilled coffee is a tough smell to get out of a car and that the odor of sour lattes would ruin the luxury car experience for me. If the salesperson had taken my issue seriously and recommended an aftermarket solution, he would have gone home with a lot more money in his commission check that day.

Most sales training programs include a mantra about *knowing thy customer.* Across the world, women are the customers who buy virtually everything there is to be sold. Women make the purchase or are the key influencers in about 80 percent of all consumer product sales in the United States alone. But who markets and sells products to women? The answer—overwhelmingly—is men, who occupy 85 percent of all Fortune 500 corporate officer positions,[2] the majority of chief marketing officer positions (nearly 70 percent)[3] and corporate executive sales management jobs, and over 90 percent of the top creative director roles at major advertising agencies.[4] They also happen to represent more than 90 percent of automotive salespeople. It's enough to make one pause and reflect on all those jokes about car salesmen. Would the jokes be different if the gender split were even? For that matter, would there still be jokes?

To make a massive generalization, men are the sex that manufactures products, and women are the sex that buys them. This is the part of the story where you may be channeling Jerry Seinfeld and thinking, *Not that there's anything wrong with that.* And you'd be right, except for one thing: most men don't understand women. (Women don't understand men either, but that is the subject for a different book entirely.) And while almost all of us will acknowledge and even joke about the gender gap in our personal lives, what's shocking is how few people have applied an understanding of gender differences to business.

This book is designed to teach you what business schools don't—how to craft your products, pitches, and marketing campaigns to cater to female buyers. Women are females first and consumers second. The ability to understand their brain structures, priorities, worldviews, and demographic patterns can provide your company with one of the most genuine competitive advantages it may ever know. And the bonus of reaching female buyers is that when it's done well, you'll make your male customers happier, too, and they won't even realize they weren't your original targets.

Forget Everything You Think You Know: Most of It Is Wrong

WOMEN weren't in positions of power when the modern corporate world was created, which means that misunderstandings about women are about as common as office cocktails on the set of AMC's *Mad Men.* The inaccurate stereotypes would almost be funny if there weren't so much money and market share at stake. Ever since the first wheel rolled out on the first assembly line, the default "gender culture" of the corporate world has been as male as a Bass Pro Shop. Men had a huge head start in the business world because they got there first. And while women are now there in such huge numbers that they're predicted to surpass men in the U.S. labor force, they got to the party so late that all the "rules" had already been set.

This means that most of the things we take for granted as conventional wisdom in marketing, sales, and product design are actually based on a male point of view. And while many companies understand that women are their primary consumers, their executive teams still go about creating products and marketing campaigns for women as if they view the world the same way men do.

Take the case of the ugly Snugli, one of the incidents that became a catalyst for this book.

The year was 2003. The place was Dayton, Ohio. I was with my former colleagues from the Zeno public relations agency at the headquarters of Evenflo Company, a baby products manufacturer that was one of our biggest clients. One of Evenflo's star products, the Snugli baby carrier, had experienced a slowdown in sales, and our team was brought in to help turn the situation around. The Snugli has a proud history as the original soft baby carrier. Worn over the shoulders, it looks like a backpack in reverse. On the day of this meeting, stiff competition from European brands, including BabyBjörn, was challenging the Snugli's position in the market. The upstarts were charging double or triple the price of a Snugli and still grabbing market share. It was time to strategize.

The Evenflo team put the Snugli in the middle of the conference table. We stared at the lump of cloth like scientists examining a new life-form. One of the Evenflo people said, "We've got to find ways to get more PR for this, or we're going to lose shelf space at our retailers."

As I looked down at the lump of cloth on the table, it was clear to me: no amount of PR would help. It was mud brown, with a pattern on the inside that looked like an old man's plaid shirt.

"It's an ugly Snugli," I told the group. "That's why it's not selling."

First I heard awkward giggles (mainly my own), and then silence. We all stared at the bulky, quilted material in front of us. Finally one of the product managers spoke.

"The important thing is that this is the safest possible baby carrier. It surpasses all Underwriters Laboratories requirements and can hold up to twenty-six pounds. It has greater tensile strength than our competitors'," said the manager. Everyone listened and nodded. The functionality of the Snugli was never in question. Not only was it strong and safe, it was practical—it had pockets, a place for keys, and sliding back straps that could be adjusted for the wearer's height.

I looked around the big table. As I'd seen so many times, every person on the agency side of the table was female, and the overwhelming majority of people on the client side were male. I had that old familiar feeling that there was a cultural misunderstanding happening in the room—a misunderstanding of gender cultures. Except this wasn't just a gender gap; it was a gender *canyon*.

So I clarified. "This is something a woman actually wears on her body, like a piece of clothing. If she's going to wear it, the Snugli should look fashionable, like any other thing she would choose to wear. It's a reflection of her taste. It needs a different style." The fabric on the Snugli wasn't just homely, it was bulky, and as any woman knows, the last thing a new mother wants to wear after childbirth is something that makes her feel even bigger.

Silence again. Then smiles. Then nods. I could almost see the lightbulbs going off above the heads of everyone in the room. What a concept—to think that because this product is worn on the body, it should be fashionable and flattering *as well as* functional. Of course! What an insight into the female mind. We all laughed at the revelation: the male-dominated Evenflo team was thinking like engineers, and we were thinking like women—their customers! The clients agreed that embarking on a new fabric design for the Snugli was the best course of action. Our team offered to draw up a list of designers that Evenflo could work with for a new style, and we soon boarded the plane home.

After that fateful meeting, we helped Evenflo partner with fashion designer Nicole Miller to create a limited edition of the Snugli as a test of the fashion-forward concept. Miller designed a sleek, unisex version of the baby carrier in black with white piping. We sent the stylish new Snugli off to celebrity moms, and before we knew it, pictures of the product being worn by celebrities, including Courteney Cox and Cate Blanchett, started appearing in glossy magazines. The company even got a thank-you note from little Apple Martin, daughter of Gwyneth Paltrow, one of the most stylish actresses anywhere.

The redesigned Snugli was selected by Oprah Winfrey as a giveaway during her "World's Largest Baby Shower" episode, and subsequently sold out online. Soon after the Nicole Miller project, Evenflo brought in a new CEO, Rob Matteucci. As a twenty-seven-year Procter & Gamble veteran and former head of Clairol, this was a man who knew from women. Matteucci embarked on a makeover for the brand, which is now fully under way.

What's different today? The company now employs women brand managers and engineers who interact directly with mothers to get feedback on Snugli designs. It has fashion directors who go to Paris and Milan for inspiration on fabrics and color trends. The lumpy cloth is a thing of the past. The brand team follows mommy blogs and website communities to stay in tune with their customers' needs and opinions. In essence, understanding women has become every employee's job.

Matteucci acknowledges it's been a long road from the bad old days of the brand, when designing from a woman's point of view was an afterthought. "The process of translating what we learn from mothers has become part of our culture, but it's something we have to work at every day," says Matteucci, who's installed a library of information about women at the company's headquarters. "We are still a work in progress. We've made strides, and we expect great things to come. Understanding women is a commitment at every level of the company, and without a doubt, it's the only way forward for our business."

If You Don't Know the Price of Milk, Read On

AFTER that Snugli meeting in Ohio, I sat on the plane thinking that if only all of our clients could see their products and campaigns through women's eyes, how much easier it would be for them to succeed. The majority of male executives I worked with had long ago abdicated shopping to their wives. I knew that when pressed, few of my clients could tell me the price of a gallon of milk. They weren't the shoppers for their households, but they spent their workdays trying to reach the people who were.

And I observed that the more senior an executive was, the more he or she made decisions about customers based on second- and thirdhand information, whether it was quantitative research reports, agency briefings, or written reports from focus groups. (Let's face it: the higher up the food chain someone is, the less likely they are to be munching M&Ms in the back of a focus group facility.) Most significant of all, the vast majority of executives were male, so they were also separated from their customers by the wide gulf of gender. Things got lost in translation. The trouble was, these smart and well-intentioned executives would assume that as long as they used women in consumer research or placed women in a few key management positions, gender differences would be taken into account somewhere along the way. Mostly they weren't.

There are many reasons for this, which we'll explore throughout the book. But one is that it isn't just men who misunderstand their female audiences. Women executives have been schooled in the same conventional wisdom of business that men have. And many find themselves going against their better instincts at work or refraining from putting forth their ideas because they don't want to cast themselves in the soft pink light of femininity, in case it's used against them.

There is no doubt: the companies who invest in understanding their primary consumer are winning. In the pages ahead, you'll learn how these companies are changing the rules, dominating their markets, and reinventing their categories. From upstarts such as method and lululemon athletica to titans like Procter & Gamble and MasterCard Worldwide, these mavericks are mastering gender differences and leaving their competitors behind. Their best practices will provide a blueprint for how you can do the same for your business.

It's not a gap, it's a canyon

Gender is the most powerful determinant of how a person views the world and everything in it. It's more powerful than age, income, race, or geography.

Most of us ignore biological differences when we examine our customer base, mainly because we've never been taught about them. The brain is still a poorly understood organ, but we do know one thing—there's no such thing as a unisex brain. New medical research has shown that brains in human beings have sexually dimorphic regions, or areas that are distinctly different between the sexes. The balance of hormones that drive our decision-making processes are complex and distinct to each sex. Biology dictates behavior in every species, whether it's muskrats, antelopes, or human beings. This book will examine the real-life implications of brain differences and their impact on women's purchasing decisions and emotional responses to product design, advertising, retail environments, and sales pitches.

Consumer research has a forest-and-trees problem

Without arguing the merits of various research methods or the fact that research is often outsourced too many levels down from corporate decision makers for them to get a handle on important nuances, one thing is true: we often overlook the obvious. Most of us have worked for companies that spend serious money conducting studies to learn about the target consumers. We'll do things like:

- Analyze their propensity to buy
- Segment them by income bracket
- Target them by age group
- Deconstruct their search patterns

- Dissect their warranty card information
- Study their media habits

We'll slice and dice data until our eyes are crossed, yet in many cases we'll overlook the one piece of information that trumps them all: *the sex of the buyer.* Considering there are only two genders in the human race and one of them does most of the shopping, it's stunning how many companies overlook the psychology of gender, when we all know that men and women look at the world very differently. It's as if the most fundamental aspect of human nature has been overlooked: *What if we are selling product X to a woman instead of a man? How does this change the equation?* The answer is that it changes the equation entirely, and far more deeply than the thin research that's so often generated. Chapter 4 will show you how Procter & Gamble developed female-centric research programs to create wildly successful products such as Swiffer that have increased the company's stock price and reenergized its standing as one of the most innovative companies in the world.

Normal depends on which bathroom you use

It's human nature to think that our own behavior is normal and that it's all those other people who are strange. Men and women inadvertently use their own gender "filters"—or personal biases—to make decisions about what they believe the other sex wants in a product, brand message, or sales environment. In a corporate world dominated by male senior executives and female consumers, the implications for misunderstandings are large and costly.

Most human drama is driven by the fact that men and

women are interested in and desire different things. What's true at home is true in business. Women respond to different tones and styles and stimuli than men do, and they assign different values to various facets of their own experience. The fact that many, if not most, major marketing campaigns go through a male "filter" before hitting the airwaves has real consequences for businesses that are trying to reach women. The lessons from companies that have successfully tapped into the female human experience, such as Master-Card, are profiled in Chapter 5.

There is a distinct female culture that decision makers need to better understand

Even though men and women live together their entire lives—as siblings, offspring, parents, spouses, friends, and colleagues—women live in a distinct female culture, with its own standards of behavior, language, priorities, and value systems, that can be as difficult for men to detect as a dog whistle.[5]

From the moment they're born, girls are socialized differently than boys, and the codes of behavior and messages they receive from adults and society are wildly different. In the pages ahead, we'll examine the fundamentals of female culture and learn why women such as Oprah Winfrey and the late Princess Diana can be considered case studies of female values. On the flip side, we'll look at how the military is a nearly perfect microcosm of male culture in action. You'll learn how to view your campaigns and communications through a new filter, to determine whether your efforts are "gender tone-deaf" when it comes to connecting with a female audience.

Five major trends drive the female demographic, and these are key to predicting consumer needs

As women increase their purchasing power almost every-where, they're unleashing major changes in society as well as in consumption patterns. These changes create needs for new products and services that are only beginning to be tapped to their fullest potential. From more women in the labor force to delayed marriages, higher divorce rates, more time spent as "singletons," and an aging population, the op-portunities are enormous for companies that understand the business implications of these demographic changes.

This book will chart the five major trends driving female populations around the world. You'll be able to use the in-formation as a blueprint for long-term planning. Each macro global trend is engendering a number of specific micro trends, which are changing women's behavior and, therefore, their needs and wants.

Life stage is more important than age

Women go through similar experiences throughout their lives, but not necessarily at the same ages. This is especially true today, when women are marrying and entering mother-hood so much later in life, and "forty is the new thirty," "fifty is the new forty," and so on. Purchasing decisions are typically based on the context of what's happening in peo-ple's lives at any given moment, not necessarily their chronological age (with the notable exception of biology-related medical products).

The old "rules" about what characterizes a forty-year-old woman, for instance, no longer apply. Today, a forty-year-old woman might have just had her first baby and is embarking on the life stage of new motherhood—which was once the province of twenty-somethings. For the next two decades, this life stage will drive her purchasing needs in a different way than is the case with other women her age, who may already have grandchildren at the same age, or perhaps no kids at all. As such, for a significant number of product categories, life stage is a more accurate gauge of a person's needs and shopping patterns than the date on a woman's birth certificate.

The knowing/doing gap

No matter how many jokes we make about the opposite sex, we continue to find our differences shocking, which is why we fail to institutionalize professional practices that account for them. The pages of this book will outline step-by-step instructions on how to approach women consumers as if they were a foreign market, because for most people, the opposite sex remains a mystery.

Case studies with senior male executives from companies ranging from Callaway Golf to Ryland Homes will prove that you don't need to be a woman to effectively market and sell to women. The chapters ahead will synthesize demographic trends, gender psychology, new research on the female brain, the wisdom of industry leaders, and field-proven business practices to give you the tools you need to create, market, and sell products to the world's most powerful consumers. Office Max, Best Buy, Sony, True Value Hardware, and even Harley-Davidson are just a few of the companies that have publicly announced female-focused initiatives. You'll learn the most common mistakes (hint: pink is not a strategy) as well as the best practices (hint: assume nothing) that you can apply immediately to your business, no matter what you're selling. This book will help you take all the fundamental truths about men and women that you've observed in your own life and apply them in a fresh way—to your business.

Now More Than Ever

Author's Postscript, September 2011

In the economic downturn that's gripped the world since this book was first published, its principles have been validated more strongly than ever. Decreased spending combined with the rising influence of social networking, social retailing, e-commerce, and the mobile Web has meant that capturing the business of women remains one of the most critical tasks for consumer-focused companies. Women dominate e-commerce spending in the majority of consumer categories, just as they do in traditional brick-and-mortar retail.[6] The tools of the trade may be changing, but women's role as "chief purchasing officer" of the home hasn't—nor have the fundamentals of female culture and biology.

It's comforting to know that no matter how fast technology advances, no matter how frequently people shop on their mobile phones and laptops, no matter how many clicks are required to make a purchase online, one thing remains the same: women are the shoppers of this world, and understanding *why she buys* is the most valuable insurance policy there is.

1

WOMEN ARE THE

MOTHER LODE

What They Didn't Teach You
in Business School

If the consumer economy had a sex, it would be female.

If the business world had a sex, it would be male.

And therein lies the pickle.

New research shows that male and female brains are so different that it's almost as if we're each living in our own gender-specific realities. You may already have suspected this—perhaps since kindergarten—but the implications for businesses are just beginning to be understood, and they are nothing short of revelatory.

Women are the driving force of the global economy, and men drive the majority of senior-level business decisions. Which means that men are usually the people who have the final say in designing and approving products that are aimed at women; developing marketing campaigns that target women; creating retail environments to attract women; and setting up sales training programs that motivate women to say, "I'll take it."

Yet when profit goals aren't met, when products aren't moving, or when marketing isn't working, it rarely occurs to executives that sex might be the problem. Not *sex* the verb, but *sex* the noun. Instead of thinking, *Perhaps we just don't understand our female customers,* people will tell themselves that the media mix wasn't right, or the distribution strategy didn't work, or the agency didn't do its job. But there is another possibility: that one sex is making its purchasing decisions differently, in a way the other just can't see.

There are some obvious reasons this can happen. From the moment we're born, gender identity is a crucial part of our personality development. Masculinity itself is often defined as *that which is not feminine.*[1] From the time they're young, boys learn to reject or repress all things feminine to be accepted by their peers and society at large, which is just one reason you don't see a lot of six-year-old boys wearing hot pink outfits to soccer practice.[2] Throughout their childhoods, boys are under pressure to prove their masculinity by shunning or even mocking feminine traits. The penalty for being viewed as even remotely feminine is to risk being humiliated for being a "sissy."

Then, after about twenty-two years of this societal pressure, many men find themselves graduating from college (and some from the über-masculine world of fraternity culture) and entering jobs in which their paycheck suddenly depends on understanding, identifying with, and selling things to women. Fresh out of business school and poof! they're a junior brand manager on a diaper product. Once on the job, few executives of either sex get any kind of formal training on gender differences. They are just expected to informally "pick up" this knowledge through colleagues and vendors. For many people in these positions, achieving success has historically involved some trial and error, lots of smarts, and just enough consumer research to be dangerous. But in a era where businesses are struggling and every sale counts, that old formula isn't enough anymore. Now, most consumer-driven companies must master female psychology to survive, because when it comes to consumer spending, women are the sex determining their fortunes. Just when executives have mastered becoming tech literate, they find there's another skill they need to keep up: becoming *female literate.*

It's a subject that can seem overwhelming when you stop and think about it. How well can the sexes ever really understand each other? The fact that we don't—and that we often want different things from life—is what drives sitcoms and drama plots the world over. It's the foundation of everything from Shakespeare's plays to my husband's insistence on setting our alarm clock to his favorite Rush song ("Limelight") every morning, just to playfully torture me. Ask any woman you know: Geddy Lee's wailing falsetto is a guy thing. Mutual incomprehension between the sexes is one of the most maddening and delightful aspects of life. But there's no room for it in business.

We don't check our biology at the door when we walk into work every morning, so the challenges we have in understanding the opposite sex in our personal lives can spill over to work without our realizing it. To plumb the depths of the gender gap for this book, I've talked to dozens of executives of both sexes, across industries. For better or worse, their stories are similar.

"The things that interest women are so strange to me," explains one male senior sales executive. "For instance, I got a new suit and wore it to the office the other day. When I got home, the first thing my wife asked me was, 'Did anyone comment on your new suit?' It was such a crazy question, because of course no one commented—I work with a bunch of guys, and nobody would ever care about my clothes, let alone say anything about them. I'm constantly mystified that my wife and her friends notice everything about everything—what other people wear and how they look, or whether they've gotten a new haircut or lost weight. Every time we go to someone's house, my wife will notice a new piece of furniture or a new picture on the wall. And when she brings it up to me, I usually have no idea what she's talking about, because I would never notice—or care."

It's easy to see how this example of the gender gap could impact a business. Been to a Sears lately? The out-of-date decor, peeling paint, and drab fixtures are just a few of the things keeping female customers away from the once-mighty retailer, which stubbornly refuses to update its stores, and has seen its stock price and market share diminish as a result. Women may notice things about your products, marketing campaigns, or sales environment that they dislike, and these are the very things that can escape the attention of management entirely or be viewed as too inconsequential to invest in. Is it common sense to take women's responses seriously? You would think so. But when men and women look at the world, they often see different things.

If women consumers are important to your business, the path to increased revenues is to listen to them long enough to hear what they have to say. Some men have told me this isn't always easy.

"When I'm around groups of women, I genuinely find it hard to listen to them for very long," confesses a male CEO, speaking on condition of anonymity. "I try, but I'm just not interested in talking about other people, or discussing who's having marital issues, or hearing about someone's emotional problems. I either leave the room or tune them out, which is something I learned to do when I was about twelve years old, growing up with sisters. My refuge was to head to the garage and build go-carts. Now I keep a pool table downstairs instead. At work, I find it hard to listen to research about women consumers for the same reason. You have to wade through so much stuff to get to the root of things. All I want to know is, 'What's the issue?' Then I can address it with a solution, get the results, and move on. But it's not easy to discover what women want, and sometimes I think we take shortcuts."

In interviews, I heard this same opinion expressed, in slightly different ways, from all kinds of businessmen. Men tend to think that women talk about *nothing,* when the reality is they talk about *everything.* I feel compelled at this juncture to acknowledge that women are often just as uninterested in, or confounded by, some of the topics of men's conversations—fantasy football, anyone?—but since it's women who dominate consumer spending, and women who determine the fortunes of so many companies, then it is women who must be understood.

It doesn't require a leap of imagination to think that if some men find it difficult to tune in to the conversations of the women they know and love, they will have the same issue at work when it comes to hearing the drives and emotional aspirations of their female customers. The innate desire of most men to avoid discussions about messy, emotional female "stuff" is what leads to shortcuts in business strategies targeting women (such as painting products pink with the presumption that it's female catnip) and the continued use of stereotypes in advertising, because it's simply easier to go those routes than to wade deeply into the female mind.

Here's the headline: if you think women's conversations are trivial, it's time to get over it, especially if you want your business to survive through a tough economy. Within the rich details of women's conversations are the road maps to what they need and want—and, ultimately, to increased profitability for your business. Women will tell you—indeed, probably have already told you—everything you need to know about how to run a business that appeals to them, but too often executives are tuned out or only listening for what they want to hear.

Take the story of two guys we'll call Trey and Steve. They're a couple of twenty-something agency creatives whose company recently won a piece of canned-food business. Trey and Steve have been assigned to come up with a new campaign targeting mothers of young children. Their strategy is to shake up the category by positioning their client's product as the hippest thing to hit canned food in years. They believe the product can be transformed by their creative powers into something aspirational. And while they would never admit it to their client, part of their strategy is driven by the thought, *If we have to work on canned food, then at least we're going to make it cool.*

The only problem is that Trey and Steve don't know anything about what drives the purchasing decisions of mothers, and quite frankly, they're not that interested. On the surface they are, but they have no real desire to go deep, because they already have their own ideas about what's cool, and being a mom isn't one of them. Trey and Steve's creative "war room" is full of ripped-out magazine pictures depict-ing their target consumer, and without exception, the moth-ers in the photos look like the kind of women Trey and Steve would like to date.

Like many young creatives, Trey and Steve are living the classic bachelor's lifestyle. Their refrigerators are empty except for the requisite "dude food": beer, cheese, and ketchup. They order takeout for dinner. The daily life of a mother with young children is as alien to them as that of a Tibetan monk. Trey and Steve have read research reports on the target audience given to them by their all-male client team, but when it comes to developing the strategy and the creative, they're relying on their gut instincts—and so are the clients who hired them.

Naturally, their gut instincts are *male*. Since their clients are also male, they think Trey and Steve's ideas are right on. They're currently embarking on a concept that's so edgy it's in danger of alienating the very women they're trying to attract. But they can't see that, because for Trey and Steve and their male clients, masculine concepts don't seem "masculine"—they seem normal.

I'll fast-forward to the end of Trey and Steve's story. After the campaign proves ineffective and doesn't "move the needle," the client will fire Trey and Steve's agency and go on the hunt for another hot shop to deliver the elusive big idea. It will never occur to any of them—to Trey, to Steve, or their clients—that the reason for the campaign's failure might have been a lack of understanding of the opposite sex.

You know the old expression that goes, "I know 50 per-cent of my marketing budget is wasted. I just don't know which 50 percent"? Here's the answer—it's the 50 percent that doesn't appeal to women.

Trey and Steve and their clients are a composite of several teams I've worked with over my agency career who were part of the inspiration for this book. I've also worked with incredibly insightful men who taught me a thing or two about tapping into people's emotions. But as of today, there are still too many executives like Trey and Steve out there, of all ages, who are out of touch with the very target audience with whom they need to connect. It's hard to blame them; the lessons they must learn are teachable, but no one is teaching them. In most businesses that rely on a predominantly female consumer base, there's no formal structure for learning about gender psychology. It doesn't appear anywhere on the organization chart, but it should. Surprisingly, women also find this gender education valuable as well, because they have been taught the rules of conventional wisdom, which are often rooted in masculine values.

Still Relevant After All These Years

SOME people think talking about gender differences is passé—just a hangover from the twentieth century. We're all equal now, right? Gender is so 1970s! Women fought the good fight in the liberation movement, they're beginning to outnumber men in the U.S. workforce, they graduate from colleges in higher numbers than men, there are (a few) Fortune 500 women CEOs, and there's Rachel Maddow on MSNBC and Hillary Clinton as secretary of state. And many men will tell you, "I'm surrounded by women at work." Right?

Well, not exactly.

The matter of the glass ceiling is not what we're here to discuss (and yes, it still exists). This book has a different goal—to help you see your business through the eyes of women, and to identify the blind spots that might be weakening your financial performance without anyone in the company realizing it. There is an unseen female culture in this world, and whether you're a man or a woman, the job of this book is to help you identify it at one hundred paces, understand it, and leverage it for mutual success—yours and that of the women you serve. In a depressed economy where women are keeping an even tighter hold on their purse strings, understanding women should be job one, because no one can afford to guess.

Women Are Females First and Consumers Second

HERE'S the rub: women are females first and consumers second. If you don't find that surprising, then here's what is— the lack of serious thought and attention that's been given to gender differences in product development, sales, and marketing, when it could be argued that these are the differences that matter most. Knowing your audience as women must be accomplished before you can begin to understand them as consumers.

Some people still need to be convinced that studying women is important, even though the knowledge that women are the world's power shoppers is so intuitive and well supported by market data, society, sitcoms, husbands, magazines, and late-night comedians. An outsider from another planet could be forgiven for assuming that most businesses conduct themselves accordingly. It would be natural to believe that executives are constantly engaged in the study of this "alpha consumer," creating products that ergonomically fit women's bodies, retail environments that appeal to female sensibilities, sales training programs that address women's speaking styles and body language, and marketing campaigns rooted in female gender psychology. All with the goal of increasing stock price and market share. Right?

Wrong.

It's human nature for people to assume that their own preferences are natural, normal, and "right" without realizing that these preferences may in fact be rooted in gender. Once you become aware of this, you'll start noticing it a lot in your personal life, as I did a few weeks ago. My husband and I were over at another couple's house for dinner when our friend suggested we watch a movie on cable—the violent, computer-enhanced film *300*. Our friend is a cultured guy who likes all kinds of movies, but this night, he wanted an action flick. When his wife and I protested because the violent scenes from the movie's advertising campaign had turned us off, he said, "Come on, it was a big hit!" and then read aloud this summary of the movie from the popular website IMDb.com to convince us:

> *When the ambitious King Xerxes of Persia invades Greece with his huge army to extend his vast slave empire, the brave King Leonidas brings his personal bodyguard army composed of three hundred warriors to defend the passage of Thermopylae, the only way by land to reach Greece. Using courage and the great battle skill of his men, he defends Thermopylae until a treacherous Greek citizen tells King Xerxes a secret goat passage leading to the back of Leonidas's army....*[3]

Goat passages? Was he kidding? We laughed out loud. We couldn't believe he thought this description would persuade us to watch the movie. It is an understatement to say it had the opposite effect. In this instance, our friend's masculine instincts about what was exciting did not match ours.

Watch Your Blind Spot

THE point of this story isn't that all women hate action movies or that all men love them, because it simply isn't true. (I myself am a huge fan of the Bourne trilogy.) The point is that sometimes words and images that can be exciting for men can cause a negative reaction in women. This is a misunderstanding that can be harmful to businesses, and you see it repeatedly in advertising—especially automotive advertising. As an example, consider the print campaign for the Ford Flex SUV. It shows a car driving through the darkness in a way that seems either scary or exciting, depending on your point of view. Here's how the copy reads:

FORD FLEX: CPR FOR THE DEAD OF NIGHT

Go stimulate something. Like the idea that a vehicle with three rows of seats can also be a nimble-footed, refrigerator-equipped, 24 mpg head-turner. Discover the strikingly original Flex at fordvehicles.com.

Now let's see. This car has three rows of seats, with capacity for seven people. It's got a fridge. It sounds like a family vehicle to me, which means that women will be buying and influencing the purchase of this car. Perhaps it would be better not to use words such as *CPR* and *dead* to headline a campaign for a vehicle in which women are going to be transporting their families. The ad is stimulating, all right, but not in a good way.

The American automotive industry is an easy target, I realize. But is there any doubt that a lack of awareness of customer preferences has played a role in its downfall? The industry is littered with ads written from a masculine point of view, even though women purchase and influence more than half the car sales in the United States and even though these ads frequently appear in women's media. The campaigns are a reflection of an automotive culture (specifically Detroit's) that clearly emphasizes masculine ideals. Models like the Yukon, Navigator, Expedition, Suburban, Hummer, Durango, Escalade, and Ram, to name just a few, are four-wheeled monuments to size and power. If you played a word association game involving the names of American cars, you'd likely come up with adjectives such as *hulking, horsepower,* and *guzzling.* If you played the same game but substituted the names of Asian imports, you'd probably hear more "feminized" words such as *small, nimble,* and *practical.* Asian cars used to be mocked by some people for these quasi-"feminine" traits, but clearly, no one is laughing now.

With a few notable exceptions, the design and marketing of American cars scream "masculine." Detroit has clearly and painfully missed the boat on changing consumer tastes in the last few decades, including female tastes. The predominantly male management teams have assumed for too long that their own values and design tastes are the same as consumers'. Only time will tell if they will recover from this near-fatal blind spot, and I am rooting for them that they will.

There Are Two Sexes in the Human Race, and One of Them Does Most of the Shopping

IT'S no secret that women make or influence the majority of consumer purchasing decisions for the home—about 80 percent in the United States. Women are the primary shoppers for their households, which means they're buying not only for themselves but also for everyone else—spouses, kids, friends, family, colleagues, and often their older parents—which multiplies their buying power and influence. If a married man needs a new pair of socks, there's a decent chance his wife will be buying them.

The gender gap in business is illustrated by the fact that men occupy 97 percent of all Fortune 1000 CEO positions,[4] the majority of top chief marketing officer positions (66 percent),[5] and nearly all the head creative director roles at the major advertising agencies (always north of 90 percent, though the exact figure depends on the day).[6] Men hold 85 percent of clout titles (those higher than vice president) in the Fortune 500.[7] Studies show that even now, women feel misunderstood and ignored by marketers. A recent body of research from the Marketing to Moms Coalition (of which I am a founder) demonstrated that nearly half of the women surveyed—46 percent—felt that marketers were not doing a great job of connecting with them. That's a lot of room for improvement, and it represents a massive opportunity for the brands that can break through their competitors' ineffective messages. As if the economic benefits of reaching women weren't compelling enough, there are social and political implications as well.

We're actually getting to a point where gender understanding might be legislated. In 2008, members of the

European Parliament voted overwhelmingly in support of a report on the negative effects of marketing on gender equality and stereotyping. Though not legally binding, the report will be used to draft new European Union legislation that calls for businesses to stop using unrealistic and sexist images of both genders in their advertising.[8] Could a lack of gender understanding eventually go from being unwise to illegal? Probably not, but this new development from Europe is certainly enough to give one pause.

As I write this, people in every conceivable industry are being challenged to create products and programs with female appeal, particularly in gender-neutral or traditionally "male" categories such as consumer electronics, insurance, finance, and, yes, automobiles. This is because women have never been more powerful in terms of their buying power. Historically, they've always had *informal* purchasing authority for their households (meaning they were in charge of shopping for it, though they often were spending their husbands' income), and they still do, but they now have the added weight of *formal* shopping authority—they're earning money themselves, and enriching their households while they're doing it.

Goodbye Bunk Beds, Hello iPods

THE entire economy has benefited from women's labor. Almost all the income growth in the United States since 1970 has come from women working outside the home.[9] Before women starting working in large numbers, America lived in a world where families had one car, one television, and one stereo, and the kids shared bedrooms as depicted so cheerfully in the popular 1970s television show *The Brady Bunch*.

Then millions of women went off into the workforce and their incomes slowly created a new norm—households with multiple cars; kids with their own rooms, television sets, and computers; each member of the household with his or her own cell phone and iPod. The mass affluence we've grown accustomed to in industrialized countries has been driven in large part by women's incomes.

In addition to increasing their households' purchasing power, women are driving consumer trends, from the mass luxury movement to the design movement to the do-it-yourself industry. And because more women than ever are running their own households (27 percent of all U.S. households are headed by a woman, according to the U.S. Census), they're often the only one in their homes making the purchasing decisions, large and small. Women are also the dominant sex earning bachelor's degrees in most of the world's industrialized countries, which means that the trajectory for their earning power will be even higher in the years to come.

The social and demographic trends impacting women around the world, which are outlined in the next chapter, are valuable insights that set the stage for what women will want and need from business over the next twenty-five years. The pages ahead are designed to do four things: first, arm you with the most current data about female buying power; second, provide you with insights into how women view the world and everything in it, including whatever it is you're selling; third, give you an overview of the most important demographic trends that will help you with long-range planning; and finally, bring the concepts of this book to life by sharing real-world case studies, with practical tips and strategies that you can apply to your own business.

Assume Nothing: No Matter Where You Live, Women Are a Foreign Country

THE easiest way to grasp female culture and use the insights to your advantage is to view it as a foreign market. Every country in the world has its own official language(s), cultural norms, and rituals. This is generally true for men and women as well. Each of us is born into an unseen and imperceptible culture built around our gender. We're so close to it that we take it for granted, and we assume the opposite sex knows all about it and understands it, too.

Not long ago, I went on a business trip to Italy. I was at a lively bar full of Italians, and there was another American in our group. He was a man in his fifties. Back in the United States it was the middle of football season, and this guy could not stop talking about his favorite team back home, the Philadelphia Eagles. He talked animatedly and at length about his favorite star players and controversial plays, none of which anyone in the room cared anything about.

As the only other American present, I was embarrassed. This guy had forgotten himself; he couldn't step out of his own culture long enough to realize that Italians—and the rest of the world, for that matter—were interested in an entirely different kind of football, and wouldn't have any reason to be interested in the gossip and inner workings of the Philadelphia Eagles. They were all clearly bored by the conversation but trying to be polite. It was a cultural gaffe—the same kind of cultural gaffe that can occur with businesses that are trying to reach women when they don't understand what really interests them and what doesn't.

Take consumer electronics as an example. Products are often sold by emphasizing technical descriptions that are meaningless to anyone other than enthusiasts, who are likely to be male. Other examples appear almost everywhere you look. Many furniture stores still schedule deliveries during business hours, which requires customers to take a day or half day off work, a decades-old practice that assumes someone in the household stays home all day. Business-to-business ads use the language of war to sell their services, finding a thousand ways to call competitors "the enemy" without realizing that kind of language turns off female executives. Customer service numbers force busy callers into irrelevant sets of options that compel them to either scream into the phone or slam down the receiver. A woman buying a BlackBerry for her new job will be handed a belt clip that she will never wear, instead of something more suitable for a female wardrobe. Every day, in virtually every industry, the gender differences of the most powerful consumers are overlooked or untapped. The good news is that the opportunities for improvement—and subsequently increased sales—are vast, and the solutions are relatively simple once you train yourself to see the world through a woman's eyes.

Seeing the Forest as Well as the Trees

LET'S stop right here and take a moment to assess the situation. Here's what we know:

- **Women drive consumer purchasing.**
  In cultures around the world, gathering provisions for the household has long been considered an important part of a woman's role. This is obvious.

- **Men dominate the senior levels of most of the companies that make and market the products women buy.**
This isn't always obvious, because there are so many women in middle management.

- **Men and women are so different, they often have trouble communicating with one another.**
This is obvious to anyone who has ever lived with a member of the opposite sex.

- **Understanding these differences can provide businesses with a significant competitive advantage, but it takes work.**
This is obvious only to those companies that are already doing it.

- **The gender gap is a source of missed opportunities and lost revenue, and it should be addressed through education and training.**
Aha. This is the part that hasn't been so obvious. Until now.

This train of thought seems simple, but there are big reasons why many companies cannot yet see the forest for the trees, nor the opportunities that can open up for them when gender differences are understood in depth.

- **Political correctness stifles frank discussion of the subject, even among women.**
Because the glass ceiling still exists, many people are uncomfortable discussing the differences between men and women at work, in all kinds of contexts. Over the past few decades, women have worked so hard to prove they're equal that they're often hesitant to point out that

they're different—just in case they're viewed as lesser or weaker. Men don't like to bring up the subject because they fear being viewed as politically incorrect at best or accused of sexual harassment at worst. Clearly, the message of this book is to celebrate, appreciate, and leverage the differences for mutual success. Pretending these differences don't exist doesn't serve anyone well and can run a business into the ground.

- **Much of the biological research on brain differences between the genders is relatively new and hasn't trickled down to either the general public or the business world.**

For most of human history, doctors and scientists assumed that all human organs were basically the same, except of course for those involved in reproduction.[10] We now know there are distinct differences between male and female brains, and that these differences impact a person's behavior and view of the world. The practical implications of these insights haven't yet had much of an impact on business. There are exceptions—Procter & Gamble, for example—where this understanding has had a measurable effect on both the top and bottom lines. As we will explore later, though, this is still an unrealized opportunity for most.

- **Gender differences are not widely taught in business courses at the undergraduate level or in MBA programs.**

The lack of recognition starts at the undergraduate and MBA levels, where behavioral implications of gender— at least when it comes to the making and marketing of products and services—are only superficially explored, if they are explored at all. Gender studies courses at universities tend to focus on social and political aspects of the subject, not the positive implications for businesses when they get it right.

- **The fish are the last to discover the ocean.**
As this old Chinese proverb implies, each gender views its own priorities and behavior as normal, and so it's easy for male decision makers to believe mistakenly that their female customers share their preferences and priorities.

The Female Economy

IT'S well known that women dominate the selection and purchase of consumer categories such as food, health and beauty, and household goods. But their power is rising in nontraditional and classically "male" categories, too, and the companies that don't recognize this are giving their competitors the upper hand. Assumptions that big-ticket items are purchased primarily by men are simply out of date. By a ratio of nearly two to one, more women than men say they make most of the decisions in their households.[11] The old stereotypes about men driving all the decisions for cars, houses, computers, and consumer electronics are no longer accurate, and the companies that view women as small-time players in these industries are in danger of losing share to those who get it. Take a look at the numbers:

APPAREL:
65 PERCENT OF PURCHASES MADE BY WOMEN.[12]

This number is high because women buy clothes for themselves, their kids, and often their husbands. Which means that no matter what you're selling, one of the important questions to ask yourself is not just "Who is my end user?" but "Who is the person who purchases my product, and is that person different from my end user?"

Automotive:
52 percent of all new vehicle purchases, including trucks, made by women (80 percent of purchases influenced by women)[13]

Women buy cars for themselves and for their driving-age children. Women also are the veto vote for cars their husbands want, but you wouldn't know it by the sheer over-load of testosterone-fueled car advertising, or by the customer service experiences at dealerships, which provide little in the way of comfort, both literally (inadequate furniture and ambience) and figuratively ("Please wait here while I go talk to my manager").

Consumer electronics:
45 percent of purchases made by women (61 percent of purchases influenced by women)[14]

Household penetration rates for men and women are nearly identical in consumer electronics, with a few exceptions, such as the fact that women buy more cell phones and men buy more navigational devices. (Is this because men won't ask for directions?) Women often use different criteria when evaluating consumer electronics, such as envisioning items in context (i.e., "Is this TV too monstrously large for the wall space in our living room?" "Is this camera too heavy for my purse?" "Will my kids be able to use this, too?") For women, context weighs heavily in big-ticket purchasing decisions.

Health care:
80 percent of family health care decisions made by women[15]

This is the "Dr. Mom" effect. Most women are the first responders to sick family members, and they assume the role of primary caregiver and health care manager to those who are ill. Even when it comes to medical products targeted to men, women are often the ones who either encourage the men in their lives to see a doctor, or buy products on their behalf. Women tend to put their family members' medical needs ahead of their own.

Travel:
70 percent of decisions made by women[16]

Whether it's Disney or Düsseldorf, women plan vacations for themselves and their families. They also make up an increasing portion of business travelers. From "girlfriend" travel packages to hotel room decor—in which items such as beds, linens, and lamps are now available for purchase via a hotel's catalog—women's preferences are driving changes in an industry that historically has catered to male decision makers.

Insurance, investments, and retirement accounts:
90 percent of women participate in decisions that affect their household's retirement and investment accounts[17]

More women in the workforce mean more women contributing to 401(k)s and other investment accounts. The twin phenomena of delayed marriages and frequent divorces also means that more women are the sole financial decision makers for their households. Women think about investing differently because the trajectory of their lives is different from men's. They spend more time out of the workforce during their lives to care for others, and they spend more years in retirement because they live longer. There tends to be a confidence gap with women, however, the majority of whom worry about the best ways to plan for their financial security.

HOMES:
20 PERCENT OF PURCHASES MADE BY SINGLE WOMEN; 91 PERCENT OF ALL PURCHASES INFLUENCED BY WOMEN[18]

Delayed marriages and high divorce rates mean that more single women than ever are investing in homes. The condo mania of the 1990s and early 2000s made it easier for many women to purchase affordable real estate. Even within couples, women are the primary decision makers in the purchase of a home. Men are simply not motivated to buy houses that their wives don't like.

WINE:
55 PERCENT OF ALL PURCHASES MADE BY WOMEN[19]

The beer industry has been trying to crack the women's market for ages, with little success. (I've heard women referred to as the "holy grail" by beer industry executives.) Women remain loyal to wine, and their participation in wine consumption has led to a host of female-friendly brands such as Red Bicyclette and Barefoot, both from E. & J. Gallo Winery.

GAMING:
40 PERCENT OF PLAYERS ARE WOMEN[20]

Gaming continues its long march into the mainstream by steadily adding more women customers. The Wii from Nintendo has made huge inroads with women of all ages, and has ingeniously brought the "other half of the population" into the world of gaming in a way that's far more appealing to them than the violent games created for young men.

Many companies have yet to effectively track their buyers by gender. Yet in virtually every category, women have buying power or influence over the product purchase. The word *influence* may sound soft, but make no mistake, it's important. It means that when a woman and her spouse make a purchase jointly, as with a new car or home, the woman is the primary influencer; if she doesn't approve of something, her husband (or her kids) probably won't get it. It works the other way around, too—if a woman wants something, she'll often find a way to persuade her husband or other family members to get it. This combination of purchasing power and influence is the reason women dominate the consumer economy.

Having Women on Your Team Is Not Enough

If you're tasked with creating something that depends on a female audience for success, it would be foolish to exclude women from your team. But I see it happen all the time. Sure, women will be in the focus groups, they'll be represented in the research reports, and sometimes they'll be in midlevel or junior positions on a team, but too often they'll be absent from the senior management teams calling the shots on the project, and that's just myopic. If you were targeting the Chinese market with a new initiative, you'd certainly want the opinions of Chinese people on your team, and the situation is similar when it comes to men and women. If you don't have strong female representation, you're in danger of missing the important nuances that will connnect you with your target. At worst, you may inadvertently offend them.

It's crucial to understand that women find themselves between a rock and a hard place on this matter. Many are hesitant to point out and defend gender differences with male coworkers, because they are in effect reminding their colleagues that they're different, and most women work hard to prove they're not.

The reluctance stems from the fact that qualities traditionally considered feminine, such as empathy and a focus on the well-being of others, are not really valued outside of the human resources department. And when they are, they're usually part of a mission statement that gets lip service only. Women don't want to be stereotyped at work or have gender biases used against them. Older women are particularly conscious that until recently they were excluded from jobs simply because of their sex. This means that both genders in the office need to be fully engaged in understanding the primary consumer. An inability to grasp and appreciate feminine qualities will keep both men and women from connecting with their target.

Genuine knowledge of women's brain structures, priorities, worldviews, and demographic patterns can provide you with genuine competitive advantages. It's time to jump on the situation before your competitors figure out that this is what they need to be doing, too.

2

A Tour of the Genders

Did you know that drowning victims are overwhelmingly male?

It's not because they don't take enough swimming lessons. Experts believe it's because boys and men have a tendency to overestimate their abilities, especially in dangerous situations. The same confidence that gave men the courage to chase ten-thousand-pound mastodons back in hunter-gatherer societies is the same instinct that gives them the confidence to swim in rough waters today, believing that nothing bad will happen to them. It is also the same kind of overconfidence that drives high-risk financial bets, as the 2008 crash of Wall Street attests. The male brain can find it exhilarating to meet danger head-on. After all, no guts, no glory.

This gender difference about male confidence, which is

clearly a generalization and doesn't apply to every individual male (especially Michael Phelps and Greg Louganis), nonetheless provides context for some of the bold business decisions we read about in the news every day. It also underscores one reason smart companies may be underperforming in their markets. Simply put, many male executives overestimate their knowledge of women consumers. They understand women on a superficial level, which they mistake as being deep—and in a female-driven economy, that's what's known as swimming in dangerous waters. Yet it's a problem easily rectified through a little education.

Here It Is: A Little Education

As we examined in Chapter 1, it's hard to be an astute and vocal observer of women's insights if you live in a society that pressures men to repress "feminine" behaviors—which arguably describes every major society in the world. If you scoff that this is old-school thinking, check out the "Get Some Nuts" British campaign from the Snickers chocolate bar brand, which features hypermasculine actor Mr. T attacking men who exhibit signs of "feminine" behavior, which apparently includes things like speed walking, yoga, going to wine bars, and moaning in pain after an injury. Astonishingly, Snickers appears to have chosen bullying as its brand platform—even in our supposedly enlightened age—proving that men are still under pressure to conceal feminine traits in public, lest they be viewed, in the words of the ads, as a "disgrace to the man race."

Men are not born knowing how to please women consumers and it can be considered emasculating to ask, given the pressures of male culture. And it can be awkward for female executives to bring up behaviors they believe men will find foolish, simply because the behaviors are perceived as feminine. Here's a simple example. A woman named Jenny is working on a project to update an insurance company's website. Her colleagues, a couple of guys, have chosen to use a stock photo of a couple sitting next to each other on a couch as one of the site's primary images. Jenny believes the photo would be more effective if it showed the couple cuddling happily, not sitting shoulder to shoulder staring straight ahead. *The couple doesn't even look like they know each other,* she thinks. Before she brings this up, however, she has to consider some of the implications of voicing her opinion.

First, she knows that even using the word *cuddling* with her male colleagues might result in good-natured ribbing at her expense, because it sounds so "girly." *Cuddling* is one of those words, such as *sweet, cute, adorable,* and *amazing,* that are associated with women and therefore rarely used by men. She can imagine their reaction: *Cuddling! You want them to cuddle?*

Then there's the chance that the conversation will turn to the topic of whether Jenny likes to cuddle at home with her husband. She doesn't want her colleagues to picture her cuddling, or to tease her about enjoying cuddling (which of course she does enjoy, and they probably do, too, though none of them will admit it). She knows that any admission of her enjoyment of cuddling may undermine her reputation as a competent executive and could have lingering effects. If she brings up something equally "girly" on the next project, she could get a reputation for being soft, sappy, and not serious.

In the end, Jenny gives her opinion but is careful about

how she does it. She doesn't use the word *cuddle,* and she frames everything from the perspective of the target audience and not as her own opinion, even though, as a professional, she is paid to make these kinds of judgment calls. Women find themselves treading carefully at work all the time, even when it comes to helping their colleagues understand what will appeal to an audience of women.

The challenge is exacerbated by the fact that until now, actionable information about brain differences and gender hasn't been widely available to a business audience. Luckily, there has been a great amount of new research that can help illuminate the differences that matter in business. This data can help both sexes overcome the perceived subjectivity and biases of ideas crafted for a female audience.

Men's and Women's Brains: As Distinct as You've Suspected

THERE'S an old joke that the brain is the largest sex organ in the body. Since the brain is the organ that drives behavior, this joke is rooted in truth.[1] In the last several years, researchers have found mounting evidence that the brain works differently in men and women and that these differences impact how each gender sees the world.[2] Gender differences come into play in just about every mammal that's been studied. These differences influence how we learn, how we play, how we fight, how we process emotions and information—and, ultimately, how we respond to business messages.

The brain is the most complex organ in the human body, and medically speaking, it's still poorly understood. All that gray matter between our ears is shaped by our genetics, biology, and culture. Arguably, women's brains are even more poorly understood than men's. For most of history, women were excluded from all manner of medical research because their hormone fluctuations, menstrual cycles, and pregnancies "interfered" with testing standards. Subsequently, the "generic" patients in medical studies of all kinds—including those of the brain—were usually male. Generally speaking, outside of the reproductive organs, women were considered smaller versions of men. It's only relatively recently—within the last three decades or so—that awareness of gender has begun to change the way medical research is conducted on a broad scale.

Back in sex education class, between all those giggles, many of us learned about hormones like testosterone and estrogen, which play a major role in driving the behaviors of each sex. But how about the biology of the brain itself? Is it different between men and women? Are we wired differently from birth? Where does nature end and nurture begin? Why do men like Rush and women like Sarah McLachlan? And what are the implications for business?

Researchers are increasingly finding that male and female brains are indeed different and that there is no such thing as a unisex brain. Imaging technologies such as positron emission tomography (PET) scans are demonstrating that brains in human beings have sexually dimorphic regions, or areas that are different between the genders. These include:

- Amygdala—Our center for emotions, fear, and aggression
- Hippocampus—The principal hub of emotion and memory formation

- Hypothalamus—Our control center for body organs and systems
- Limbic system—The part of the brain that produces emotions
- Visual cortex—The part of the brain that processes visual information
- Corpus callosum—Our transmitter of brain signals, which connects the left and right sides of the brain

Consumer research is a vital part of any business, but sometimes it merely shows us the tip of the iceberg. To truly understand what drives the behaviors and motivations of women consumers, it's important to go deep into the biological differences that impact how they view the world. The full extent of our brain differences is still uncharted territory, but here's what scientists have determined so far:

- **Emotion.** The limbic system, or emotional bonding center of the brain, tends to be larger in women, which may explain why women are the primary caretakers for children and the elderly in almost every society in the world.[3]

- **Memory.** The hippocampus (the hub of emotion and memory formation) is larger in the female brain, which is likely the reason that women are better at expressing emotions and remembering the details of emotional events than men are.[4] This is why women can recall every word of a major argument or special event, even years later, often to the chagrin of their partners.

- **Speech.** Women use both sides of their brains for speech, while men use one. Women also have more nerve cells in the left half of the brain, the seat of our ability to process language. This may be why women find verbal communication easier than men do, and tend to have richer vocabularies.[5] (When was the last time you heard a man use the word *mauve?*) Men tend to be more to the point in language.

- **Sex.** Men have more than twice the brain and processing power devoted to sexual drive that women do. At puberty, boys develop twenty times as much testosterone as girls do.[6] Among other things, this is a biological explanation for why the worldwide pornography industry is supported almost entirely by the male sex (in case you were wondering).

- **Socializing.** Testosterone has been shown to decrease talking as well as interest in socializing, except when it involves sports or sexual pursuit.[7]

- **Multitasking.** Women have more connections between the two sides of the brain, which may explain why they're able to do things like make pancakes while composing an e-mail. Men tend to activate one side of their brain when processing information, which means that they are better at compartmentalizing data and addressing one thing at a time before moving on to the next.[8]

- **Body language.** Women have a greater capacity to read faces and hear emotional cues in voices, which may be an evolutionary adaptation that's enabled them to respond successfully to the needs of wordless infants.[9] Women are good at this because survival of the species depends on it.

- **Spatial problems.** Women and men use different strategies to solve spatial problems. When trying to find their way, women prefer to use landmarks (turn right at the McDonald's), while men prefer to use "Euclidean information," which is why they reach for maps.[10]

These are just some of the biological explanations for behaviors we've all observed our entire lives. It's fascinating to consider that the hardwiring of our brains is what controls our reaction to business messages. In the pages ahead, we'll deconstruct what that means.

When discussing brain differences, it's important to realize that biology is just part of the equation. We're not captive to our brains. Our personal experiences and interests can actually modify the structure and function of our brains.[11] Think of our bodies—if we're overweight and out of shape, we can change that condition through our own free will. The same concept applies to our brains. If you've spent five years learning to speak Mandarin Chinese, for instance, you've effectively modified your brain circuits. These modifications also happen early in life, when we learn the social codes for our gender. From the moment we're born, parents, teachers, and all the other adults who raise us provide instructions on what is and isn't appropriate behavior. As a teenager, for instance, I learned that I'm not supposed to chew tobacco and spit it into old soda cans in public— which is something the boys at my Texas high school did all the time. There are a million of these little rules that we learn along the way, and most of them we take for granted.

Culture impacts our notion of gender enormously. Adult and peer expectations play an especially important role in shaping our brain circuits.[12] So do the media, from James Bond movies to the ubiquity of celebrities like Pamela Anderson and Paris Hilton. Biology and culture both impact how the brain develops over time, yet we still have the power to evolve our brains and our ways of thinking. In the 1960s, few people would have believed that the United States would ever elect an African American president and *almost* elect a female president. Over time, enough people's minds were opened—and for many, changed—to make the presidency of Barack Obama a reality in 2009.

In a nutshell, our gender differences impact how our brains see the world. *Sex matters.* What it means for decisions about everything from product development to marketing and sales can be summarized in the five differences outlined in the next part of this chapter. The only caveat is that these male and female behaviors are generalizations. The human race is infinite in its variety, and there are of course people who are exceptions. But these common traits provide an inportant baseline for determining the needs and wants of women. Few people have looked at the correlation between gender and business strategy. My goal is to do this in a way that helps you serve the world's most important consumers more effectively.

♛ GENDER DIFFERENCE #1 ♛

Women and men define achievement in different ways. Men strive to be independent; women strive to be indispensable.

Let's start at childhood, where gender differences reveal themselves early, much to the amazement of parents who have children of different sexes.

Consider how kids play, which has been studied in great

depth by sociologists. When little girls get together, their games are based on role playing, and scores are generally not kept. You can't win a game of tea party. Girls will play games such as house, doctor, mommy-baby, school, and grocery store, and they'll also play nurturing games with dolls. Organized sports come into their lives later on, through formal leagues run by adults. When left to their own devices, it's rare to see groups of little girls forming themselves into competitive teams.

An emphasis on nurturing and fairness is the foundation of girls' role-playing games. Girls take turns, because that's the fair way to play—"I'll be Mommy first, then it's your turn." One-on-one friendships dominate their lives, in a pattern that will continue throughout adulthood.[13] Little girls tend to have a best friend, and they can often be seen with a cupped hand over their friend's ear, telling each other their "secrets." Conversations are the glue that binds their friendships, from a very early age.

"Bossy" girls are criticized and put in their place by both peers and adults.[14] Young girls are taught that they should always be modest, that showing off is a bad thing, and that fairness is the most important part of any game. In addition, girls learn early that it's important for them to develop two social talents: being liked and being helpful. Subsequently, when they grow up, they aspire to be liked and helpful to the point of being indispensable.

This is reinforced by biology. As we've learned, in female brains, the limbic system—the emotional brain—tends to be larger than in men's. This larger limbic system makes it easier, and subsequently more important, for women to bond with other people throughout their lives.

On the other side of the playground, things are different. When little boys grow old enough to play with others, they're socialized within the context of games that are competitive and have winners and losers.[15] Through these games and sports, young boys learn about life's "rules," which is why grown men are so comfortable using sports analogies to describe them later in life. Boys strive to achieve status within their groups by dominating others, whether it's through their size and physical prowess (it's always better to be the biggest and strongest boy), their ability to issue commands, or their skill at a particular sport or subject.

Adults often view little boys who dominate others as having leadership qualities. Instead of being viewed as "bossy," as the girls are, these boys are considered natural leaders. "Look at how the other kids follow him around!" adults will say admiringly. "He's a natural leader!" Right from the start, boys are taught that independence is a virtue, and their self-esteem is fueled by achieving things without help from anyone else. Being independent, competitive, and dominant are qualities that are encouraged in boys.

All Grown Up but Still the Same

FAST-FORWARD to adulthood. Women want to achieve success in life just as much as men do, but their definition of success is different. Achievement is something more internal, and not necessarily tied to external factors such as beating someone else. That's why hypercompetitive messages in advertising typically don't resonate with women. When women compete, they compete against themselves. They

are their own toughest critics. And because they're socialized to be helpful growing up, the thought of beating others
through their own "victories" can make them feel a little
uncomfortable. After all, if you're beating someone, you're
not being very helpful, are you?

That's why women find success much sweeter if it also
benefits the people they care about. Their view of achievement is not only internal but also inclusive. With their larger
emotional center in the brain, creating successful relationships is an important priority. There are a lot of corny
stereotypes out there about women and relationships, but
the fact is that the world is built on relationships and women
are the undisputed champs at creating them. Women consider building relationships to be the most valuable of life's
achievements.

For some reason, this value of cultivating meaningful relationships is often dismissed as "women's territory" and
doesn't get much respect. It's the Rodney Dangerfield of
women's stereotypes. The irony is, most successful executives would say that their business relationships are among
their most valuable assets. If an entrepreneur wants to sell
his or her company, what people are buying is usually the
client list. (*Clients,* of course, is just another word for people
with whom one has built relationships.)

Women prioritize and cultivate strong personal and
business relationships, because creating these networks of
family, friends, and colleagues is a primary source of joy
and fulfillment. Anthropologists believe this is one reason
women handle retirement better than men: they've built a
network of relationships and friendships they can fall back
on after their working days are over. This is also the reason
that people with aging parents worry when their elderly

mother dies before their father. The common fear is that the father will spend his days alone in the dark, watching TV and eating canned food, since his wife was the one who kept up the hustle and bustle of the social relationships.

Now quick, answer this question: why don't men like to stop and ask for directions? It's the oldest cliché around . . . because it's true. Men hate asking strangers for directions because they want to figure out how to get to their destination *on their own.* This notion of succeeding independently is an important value in male culture and for many men the definition of what achievement is all about.

Men think asking for help is weak and an option to be used only when desperate. Women think asking for help is smart and a great time saver.

Men are hesitant to ask others for help—even strangers at gas stations who could provide some friendly directions— for two reasons. The first is because "they don't know they're lost," says Dr. Daniel Amen, a clinical neuroscientist and brain-imaging expert. The second is because they feel it puts them in a weakened position. It's what the pioneering linguistics professor Deborah Tannen calls the "one-down" position: when you feel you are of lower status than some- one else. Sociological research shows that men are far more status-oriented than women. They are conscious of their place in the hierarchy of the male kingdom. For proof, look no further than the military. It's the ultimate example of male culture in action.

I'm the oldest of five daughters raised in a military fam- ily, and my interest in gender stems partly from the fact that I grew up in the testosterone-fueled world of army bases. Each military base is a small, male-dominated universe that revolves around hierarchy, rituals, pomp, and circumstance.

Military protocol—arguably the precursor to modern corporate culture—is driven entirely by one's rank, which is just another word for status. Anyone who has a higher rank than you is called your "superior," and your interaction with others is strictly dictated by your place in the pecking order. I watched my father's behavior change from commanding to subordinate depending on the rank of the person he was talking to. He was adjusting his behavior constantly, and so was everyone else. It took me years to figure out the codes of behavior, and to understand why he wasn't the same person at home and when he was out mixing with other soldiers.

This notion of hierarchy exists throughout the male kingdom (even in animals, hence the term *alpha male*). Whether they're sanitation workers or chief executive officers, men are innately conscious of being in a "one-up" or "one-down" position in any given situation.[16] This fuels a competitive drive to hide vulnerabilities that could lessen their status in the eyes of others. Rising above vulnerability in all aspects of life is a fundamental principle of male culture, which is reinforced by movie and TV characters all the time. Women, on the other hand, proactively seek help and input from others. Sometimes they even ask for help when they don't need it, just to make someone else feel good.

In a nutshell, if men measure self-worth by achieving status and doing so independently, women measure self-worth by the quality of relationships they've established in their lives, starting with their own families.

For Men, Help Is a Four-Letter Word

THESE kinds of gender differences impact how people shop. I saw this in action recently at an old-fashioned hardware store. A young woman was shopping with her husband in the plumbing section. One of the old guys who worked there came shuffling down the aisle. The woman stopped him, motioned to her husband, and asked the employee where they could find size D batteries.

The man in the apron pushed up his thick glasses, ignored the woman, looked directly at her husband, and said, "You're looking for batteries? Do you know you're in the plumbing aisle?"

The husband shot a look of disgust at his wife, said curtly, "We don't need any help, we're fine," and waved the man off.

Then he turned to his wife. "You made me look like an idiot in front of that guy!"

She looked startled. "But we already looked for the D batteries and couldn't find them—what's the big deal? That's what the guy is here for!"

Her husband shot back, "I can't believe you humiliated me like that," and strode off without a backward glance, leaving her standing in the middle of the aisle.

Without realizing it, she had emasculated her husband. In his mind, she made him look stupid in front of another man. The fact that this happened with a perfect stranger who was theoretically a subordinate (an employee hired to serve customers) made no difference. The husband looked like he didn't know what he was doing in a bastion of manliness—a traditional hardware store—and that was cause for humiliation. Asking for help would have been a last resort for him, not a point of entry. He was happy to search for the product on his own, even if it took longer to do so.

And that's why the notion of a man making it all the way to the top, as his own man beholden to no one—think Clint Eastwood—is the ultimate idea of success in masculine culture. You'll start noticing that men's magazines and mass-market advertisements (particularly automotive and consumer electronic ads, and those big lighted ads you see at airports) bear this out. In parallel, you have the phenomenon of stores cutting back on employees to save money but not realizing this may be driving away their women customers, who want human help. Like the young woman in the hardware store, women view asking for help as an efficient way to get something done. This kind of gender difference drives our preferences in where and how we want to be sold things.

Women are more likely to seek human interaction in almost any type of transaction. In a recent Wharton/Verde Group study, researchers found that women react more strongly than men to personal interaction with sales associates. The study reveals that for women, "lack of help when needed" is the top problem (29 percent). Funny enough, men react more strongly to the utilitarian aspects of the shopping process, ranking "difficulty in finding parking close to the store's entrance" as the number one problem (also 29 percent).[17]

At its simplest, business is all about motivating people to buy something from you instead of from someone else, or instead of nothing at all. Clearly, understanding what motivates women is critical if they are your target audience. For example, women generally don't enjoying wading through highly technical instruction manuals, which is one of the reasons the Geek Squad from Best Buy has become so popular. For a lot of men, reading the manual and figuring out a product is part of the fun. From the time they're young, boys enjoy taking things apart, putting them back together again, and figuring out how things work. This is not as common for women. When they buy something, they usually just want the thing to do what it's supposed to do, right away.

American Airlines has a wonderful feature on its website that demonstrates a great grasp of this concept. When you go online to book a reservation (remember, women make most of the travel decisions), a little window pops up with a picture of a woman wearing a telephone headset, accompanied by the words "Need help? We'll call you back right now." If you need some live assistance from the airline, you can simply type in your phone number and an agent calls you back in about thirty seconds. It's the perfect execution of personal help in an online environment—the living embodiment of high-tech and high-touch.

The business implications for these gender differences can be summed up as:

- **Think twice before using "masculine" competitive messages in your marketing.**
  Women's definition of achievement is internal and doesn't necessarily involve beating or destroying anyone else. It's surprising how often this competitive messaging turns up, even when it has nothing to do with the product or service in question. Recently I saw a large business-to-business ad at New York's LaGuardia Airport, featuring a giant sumo wrestler facing off with a man in a business suit who was poised for a fight. It was an ad for a company that sells translation services and other types of

staffing support for companies entering global markets. Why would anyone feature two men locked in a battle pose for a company that's supposed to be helpful with multicultural issues? It's a non sequitur. The lesson is, don't see aggression where it doesn't exist.

• **No matter what your business, strive to make service a major differentiator.**

The cliché that good help is hard to find is still true, and great service can provide a serious competitive advantage when it comes to serving women. Women want assurance up front that your company won't leave them high and dry if something goes wrong. They have a highly developed sense of fairness and expect the companies they deal with to have it, too.

• **Leverage the word-of-mouth power that women customers have on any business.**

Women want to be considered indispensable, and that means being the source of valuable information to the people they care about. If women are happy with your business, they are delighted to tell people they know— especially if you provide an incentive for them to do so. From loyalty programs to referral programs, if you're not leveraging your base of women customers to bring in their contacts, you're leaving money on the table. To ingratiate women to your company, let them feel like insiders when it comes to news and information about your business. Women like to be in the know, because they enjoy being the source of good information in their social and business circles.

- **Invest in human help.**

Women believe that asking for help is an efficient way to get something done, and they won't hesitate to ask for something if you make help available to them. It's impossible to know how many women have walked out the door or abandoned a website simply because they couldn't find the help they needed in an easy or a timely fashion. Too much is better than too little.

♔ GENDER DIFFERENCE #2 ♔

Women connect with each other by talking about their feelings and revealing their vulnerabilities. Men connect with each other by engaging in activities and hiding their vulnerabilities.

At the root of women's relationships is the ritual of sharing feelings, fears, and vulnerabilities, or what's called *self-disclosure*. (Men sometimes call this *yakking*.) This is why women talk on the phone for so long or have lunch for three hours on a Saturday afternoon. I've noticed that my husband starts giving me the eye after I've spent just twenty minutes on the phone with one of my sisters or girlfriends. In his mind, twenty minutes is about nineteen longer than necessary. When I start to feel bad that I'm not paying attention to him, I begin the slow process of hanging up. What he doesn't realize is that, given the chance, I could easily go on for much longer. There is simply not enough time in the day to chat with our girlfriends about all the subjects that need to be covered.

So what do women talk about? Everything. There is no subject too small, no observation too minute. But mainly we talk about how we feel about things. Conversations about emotions are the stuff that binds women together throughout their entire lives. Women actively seek out the counsel of friends and family members for help with their problems and as a way of connecting with one another. The strange thing is that women feel powerful when they can give advice and help people with their problems—not just when they can boss them around. (For reference, see any episode of *The Oprah Winfrey Show.*)

Biologically, women have high levels of oxytocin, which is a "bonding" hormone that's triggered by intimacy. Sharing secrets and connecting in an intimate way actually activates the pleasure centers in a woman's brain. Physiologically, it feels great to bond with other women—that's one reason the phone calls are so long![18] Most men don't have tolerance for the level of detail involved in women's conversations.

Women also have a habit of getting personal fast. On a flight from Austin to Dallas I sat next to a woman who was a perfect stranger. By the time the short flight was over, I knew all about her struggle with infertility and her decision not to adopt a child from China. An extreme example of self-disclosure? Sure. Was I surprised? Not really. Women, and American women in particular, are known for talking about their feelings quite openly. And they enjoy the opportunity to connect with someone else, no matter how briefly. The woman on my flight was an extreme case, but she was clearly looking for validation from me—a stranger—that she had made the right decision about her fertility options. Somehow these conversations never happen to me when I sit next to a man, especially in business class.

From the time they are little girls, talking about feelings is the linchpin of women's relationships. Prick up your ears at the office and listen to what you hear. If a woman is having a bad hair day or feels like she's put on five pounds, she will tell all her female colleagues before they even have a chance to notice.

In female culture, a woman reveals a weakness knowing full well that the woman she's talking to will make her feel better by telling her that no, her hair really looks great today, and those pants truly do look loose. Women depend on these responses and are stricken when they make these remarks in front of men who either agree with them (not the answer they are looking for) or stay silent because they don't understand how the female conversational ritual is played out.[19] Here's how it works:

I put myself down.
You pull me back up.
You put yourself down.
I pull you back up.

That's the cadence of female communication.

My turn to make you feel good.
Your turn to make me feel good.
Everybody gets a turn.

And as you've no doubt witnessed on Monday mornings at the office, compliments are one of the most powerful ways that women connect with each other. Women use compliments as verbal shortcuts to make someone else feel good. "Did you get that new blouse this weekend? It's gorgeous!"

Female friends have been known to pass hours in conversation complimenting, reassuring, and validating one another while downing coffee and listening to each other's problems.

Why are women so prolific with their compliments? Society tells women that one of their biggest jobs is to look beautiful. This not-so-subtle message is borne out in magazines, advertisements, videos, movies, television shows, and virtually every other medium, visual or not. (How many times has the word *hot* been used in a song?) Appearance is one of the primary things that women are judged on, and so they appreciate hearing reassurances that they're making the grade. All women intuitively understand this, and subsequently provide each other with reassurances in the form of compliments. Men are often oblivious to this pressure, because they're judged on other criteria besides their looks and bodies. Have you ever heard of a bathing suit cover-up for men? No, of course not. Men aren't taught to be ashamed if they don't have a perfect body. Women are. Which explains why men are bewildered by women's endless compliments, and why women seek them out.

Female friendships are a critical and somewhat overlooked aspect of women's lives. An afternoon with the girls can make a stressed-out female feel like a new woman. This is because of oxytocin, that pleasure-enhancing chemical in the body that's released any time women are under stress, as well as when they're with the people they care about.[20] Each positive interaction with friends becomes like a mini high. Women actually have a physiological reaction to being with good friends and hearing all the laughter, supportive words, and compliments, and this is heightened when touching and hugging are involved.

The best part about receiving compliments is that they work equally well whether given by your best friend or the stranger standing next to you in the grocery store. It's all about affirmation and rationalizing each other's decisions: *"Yes, Christie, that haircut really does work on you."* And when it comes to buying products, especially big-ticket items, women look for help rationalizing everything from a haircut to a new car.

In female culture, affirmation and appreciation are closely related. Women are the queens of the thank-you gesture, and options for displaying their gratitude know no bounds. The world of thank-you notes, thank-you gifts, and thank-you bouquets is the domain of the female sex. Gratitude is given enthusiastically, with exclamation points, even for the smallest of acts: "Oh my God, thanks for picking me up this morning, you saved my life!" You can be sure that the gender that displays gratitude on such a large scale expects it in return when they give their business to a company. They often end up disappointed, which is why it can be such a competitive advantage if you put even the smallest effort into an appreciation program.

The Oprah Effect

IT's hard to think of someone who connects with women more effectively than Oprah Winfrey. She relates to women of every demographic in three powerful ways: through affirmation, through self-disclosure, and through compliments. Oprah never invented anything; she has no factories; there are no trucks loaded with her inventory cruising down the highways. Her fortune and her influence have come from her ability to connect with women. Like the late Princess Diana, Oprah publicly reveals her struggles, her vulnerabilities, her fears, and her deepest dreams for the future. She is constantly trying to improve. Women around the world think, *Wow, Oprah is just like me; she struggles with the same things I do.*

When you think about it, Oprah's fan base of moms from middle America has very little in common with this brilliant media mogul, who is single, childless, and a billionaire to boot. It doesn't matter that Oprah's fans don't have anything in common with her *on the surface.* Like most successful female-to-female relationships, it's what's below the surface that counts. Oprah works hard to minimize her status differences with her audience, which is the opposite of how male culture works. This is one of the things that make Oprah such a great salesperson—of herself, and of the values, people, and products she endorses. She simply makes women feel good about themselves, no matter what subject she's discussing. Her message is, *You're a great person.* Everything she does says, *We're all the same.* She's an extreme personification of female culture in the same way that Donald Trump is an extreme personification of male culture. Take a look at the cover headlines from an issue of *O, The Oprah Magazine,* which is all about empowerment, affirmation, and juicy storytelling, to see what I mean:

- *"You Are an Excellent Woman!" How to finally let that message seep into your bones*
- *Makeover! Is your hair color working for you—or against you?*
- *And THEN What Happened? Get swept away by 8 riveting, true stories—a wife and a knife; the shocking phone call; lost life, new life ... and more*

- *The Perfect Summer Dinner Party, Period.*
- *She's 48 and Starting to Date—A post-divorce wardrobe plan*

Can you imagine these empowering headlines on a men's magazine? *"You Are an Excellent Man!"*

No. This kind of affirmation is a woman's game. Readers are supposed to feel better about themselves after reading Oprah's magazine. It's like having lunch with a good friend, without the lunch or the good friend. The motto of the magazine is "Live your best life." It's a *helpful* slogan that resonates, because women know they are supposed to be helpful, and they genuinely enjoy receiving help, too.

Many men are mystified by Oprah's allure because they can't imagine how the act of continually revealing one's inner thoughts and vulnerabilities could be attractive to anyone. When men get together, it's never just to sit around and talk. And it's certainly never to sit around and talk about *feelings*. Men get together to *do* something, whether it's to play a game, watch other people play a game, or go to a bar. And when they talk, personal problems are not on the agenda. Men just want to relax with each other; they don't want to talk about their problems with other guys, because it would just make them feel worse.

A few years ago, my husband's best friend, Bruce, was going through a divorce. I didn't know Bruce's wife very well, and I couldn't get any information from my husband on exactly why the divorce was happening. It was driving me crazy. No matter how much time these two men spent together, the subject of Bruce's divorce never seemed to come up. So when my husband and Bruce went to Las Vegas for a weekend during the NCAA Final Four tournament, in which they were going to share a room at the Bellagio, I thought, *After they spend this weekend together, I'll finally find out what's going on between Bruce and his wife.*

When the trip was over, I picked up my husband at the airport and immediately asked him, "So what's the real reason they're getting divorced?" His mouth dropped open and he looked at me like I had antlers. He said, "We didn't talk about that—it would have ruined the whole weekend!"

If it had been two women in the room that weekend and one of them was going through a painful divorce, you and I both know they wouldn't have talked about anything else. They might not even have come up for air.

The differences between male and female communication styles are easy to see when you look for them. Check out the cover blurbs on the issue of *Men's Journal* that hit my mailbox a short time after I picked up the issue of *O, The Oprah Magazine:*

- *Lance: The Relentless Drive of America's Alpha Bachelor*
- *NASCAR Bad Boy Tony Stewart*
- *Death to Sportswriters!*
- *Inside the Quarterback Factory*
- *Best Beers 2008*
- *Great Fall Adventures*

Words such as *alpha, bad boy, death,* and *beer . . .* this is the language that sells men's magazines. *Men's Journal* is tame compared to the so-called lad magazines, such as *Maxim* or *Stuff,* which throw around words like *hottielicious* and have the wet-bikini images to back them up. Next time you're at a bookstore, head over to the magazine aisle to compare male and female cultures in all their glory. It's an exercise in which everything we know intuitively becomes gleefully obvious. In male culture, the entire world is a stage in which men compete for women, success, and victory. In women's culture, the entire world is a community, where people connect with one another to help others realize their potential inside and out, and to make life happier for everyone.

These gender differences have business implications for everything from sales training to client service, from call-center scripting to consumer research, and from advertising copy to public relations programming.

- **Empathy is an effective sales tool.**

Disclosing vulnerabilities can bond salespeople to their women customers. Saying something like "I remember the first time I installed this computer program—I found it confusing, too" can immediately make a woman feel comfortable. This is the reassuring style of communication that women use with each other in conversation. The technique is especially powerful when it comes to complex and expensive purchases such as insurance policies, new homes, cars, mortgages, consumer electronics, and financial services.

- **Validation and affirmation help women say yes.**

Being a shrewd buyer is a form of status for women. ("I *never* pay full price!") And more than men, women need help justifying their purchases, especially when it comes to products they consider indulgences. Women tend to feel guiltier than men when spending money on themselves. Help women justify buying your product or service by actively validating their decision through words and images. LG Appliances has been running a clever campaign that gives women permission to upgrade their appliances even when their old machines are working just fine. The ads show humorous fantasies of women bulldozing, sledgehammering, and otherwise destroying the unstylish old appliances in their homes. The message of the ad is, *We give you permission to get rid of that old hunk of junk, even though it's still working!*

• **Humanize your company by minimizing status differences and leveraging a sense of humor.**

Apple has successfully humanized technology products through intuitive design. Best Buy's Geek Squad has humanized IT support through its people-powered business model and self-deprecating use of the word *geek,* not to mention its use of quirky Volkswagen Beetles as its fleet. MasterCard has humanized the faceless credit-card business through its "Priceless" marketing campaign, which is inherently self-deprecating, since it admits that there are some things that its credit card just can't buy.

• **Demonstrating appreciation is one of the simplest ways to generate word-of-mouth publicity and repeat business from women.**

Show your appreciation to women customers and clients early and often. Women are the thank-you people of this world. You can bet they notice when a thank-you hasn't been given to them. They prefer to give their business to the companies that demonstrate appreciation for it, and in return they are more likely to talk about you with their friends and colleagues.

Women have a higher verbal fluency than men. They focus on the details and will talk about their love of a product or service to their friends.

Just when you thought I was done talking about women and talking, there is yet another point to make. (Remember that for women, a conversation is never really over; it is merely to be continued.) There are two primary reasons why women love a good chat, and both are related to how their brains are wired. As we've seen, women have more nerve cells in the left half of the brain, the part that processes language. They also have a greater degree of connectivity between the two parts of the brain, which may be why women find it easier than men to listen to and make speech.[21]

So how different are men and women in conversation? For one thing, women relish the details of any story; men prefer the top-line summary. Details about people are often boring to men, who find details about things more interesting—whether it's a new computer, a new car, or a sports team. In a nutshell, men are interested in how things work, and women are interested in what something will do for them. Rather than wonder about a new side-by-side freezer's volume in cubic feet, a woman will ask, "Can I fit a frozen pizza in it?"

Unlike men, women feel a sense of urgency, even obligation, to tell people about a new product or service they've discovered. It's almost an imperative in female culture. It goes back to women wanting to feel indispensable—they enjoy being the bearer of tidings that may help improve the lives of friends or family members in some small way. Notice that if you compliment a woman's outfit, her first response often will be just one word: the name of the store in which she bought it. This is her shorthand way of telling someone how he or she can get the look, too. It works something like this: "Stacy, I love your dress." Response: "Bloomingdale's!" Even though the answer is only the name of the store, it conveys, *I got it there and you can, too!*

Usually this one-word answer is followed by a much longer story detailing how the outfit came to be. If you compliment a woman, be prepared to hear the back story about whatever it is you just complimented. It's almost impossible for her to just thank you and walk away. (If you're a woman, try this. It requires the strength of ten men.) Women need to give you the details: "You know, I bought this to wear to my son's first communion, but then I thought, hey, this is perfect for work, too, so now I can wear it to the office!"

When telling their friends about a product or brand they love, women gravitate to details that demonstrate uniqueness. "This scarf is made of 100 percent bamboo. Bamboo! Can you believe it?" Such details give women what they consider to be a worthy nugget of information to pass on to their friends.

Some of the business implications of this gender difference include:

- **Don't lead with how something works—lead with the practical benefits.**
Women aren't usually as interested in the guts of something as men are. They're interested in the practical applications and the broader context of the purchase. Don't just answer the questions about what it is; talk about where they're going to put it, how they're going

to use it, and how it will affect the other people in their lives. For instance, let's say you're selling a sofa bed. Instead of promoting just the technical aspects, such as the coil count of the mattress, you could talk about context: "Spending money on a great sofa bed like this means you could transition a guest room in your home into something more useful, like an office or a media room, and your guests will *still* be comfortable." Now that's practical!

- **Use stories to bring your service to life.**

Women respond to stories more than they do to just product information. In fact, you'll notice that women will often answer questions with a story. This is a great technique for marketing (see MasterCard's "Priceless" campaign, described at great length in Chapter 5), as well as for account executives who want to up-sell customers. Tell a story of how other people have used your product or service, or paint the picture of a scenario in which women could picture themselves using it.

- **Leverage third-party endorsements and testimonials.**

The third-party credibility of having your product or service endorsed by a trusted source is often more valuable than advertising. Women trust credible experts, including their favorite magazines and bloggers, to "edit" options for them across a wide number of categories, which makes public relations an essential tool for companies reaching out to women. The explosion in consumer-opinion websites such as TripAdvisor.com, not to mention the proliferation of product and lifestyle arbiters like CNET.com and coolhunting.com, are driving brand choice across a wide range of industries. When you have happy customers, actively encourage them to post their opinions on these kinds of sites as well as on social networking sites like Facebook.

♛ **GENDER DIFFERENCE #4** ♛

Women have better memories for the details of both pleasant and unpleasant experiences. Scientists attribute this to the fact that women have a larger hippocampus — the seat of memory and learning in the brain.

For better or worse, women notice everything.

Women are wired to pick up on the details of people, places, and things—but mostly people. After all, women cater successfully to the biggest nonverbal constituency in the world: babies. Women have to notice every detail about their infants to keep them alive. They need to determine whether they're hungry or gassy, sick or just hot, happy or uncomfortable, wet or dry, full or distracted. They must use all their senses to figure them out, to continue their ancient role in the survival of the species.

Thousands of years of successful mothering means that females in the human race are finely tuned detail-noticing machines. It's this well-developed sense of reading meaning into body language, smells, sounds, and temperature changes that makes women notice everything about your business, even when they'd rather not. Blame it on estrogen. During a stressful event, the hormone activates a wider field of neurons in the hippocampus (where memories are made), which causes women to experience unpleasantness in greater and more vivid detail than men.[22]

I have a dream of running a chain of gas stations that would feature the cleanest and most comfortable restrooms in the country. I'd put up big billboards all over America's highways, advertising the sparkling bathrooms. If you don't think they're important, you're probably not a woman, and you probably don't have kids. Here's an illustrative story from one young mother of two:

> I make my trips to the grocery store quickly, because if my youngest child needs to go to the bathroom, she can't hold it. To get to the bathroom at my grocery store, you have to go through the loading dock, then down a cement staircase, then through the employee locker and break room, to the furthest crevice in the basement, to get to a dirty, two-stall bathroom.
>
> It seems like stores are investing a lot to make themselves look better and encourage you to stay in them longer, but they keep forgetting about the bathrooms. They invest so much in the checkout line—like all those flat-screen monitors at the registers—and nothing in the actual experience. When my child has a meltdown, there's nowhere to go. There's one tiny bench in the whole place, right by the front door. They'll even cram a bank in there before they'll give you a bathroom. It's clear that no one is thinking these things through, and yet every other person in the store is shopping there with their kids.

As this story illustrates, bathrooms are just one example of the details that women notice in a business establishment. But they are an important demonstration of the kind of detail that may escape the attention of men, who may have a higher tolerance for poor bathrooms. These days, bathrooms in particular are more important than ever, because of our penchant for drinking liquids everywhere we go. Coffee used to be something you drank only at home or in a restaurant, and so was water—unless it came from a fountain. Now our propensity to drink all day, every day, is such that even strollers come with matching drink holders—one for the parent and one for the baby. Whether it's Starbucks, Aquafina, or a sippy cup full of milk, what goes in must come out. And if women know they can't count on a clean bathroom, they may cut a shopping trip short or take their business elsewhere.

It's not just retail, and it's not just bathrooms. Women will notice if a salesperson's desk is messy; if there's a funny smell in the room; if employees seem to dislike each other; if the receptionist is rude; if the hold time for a customer service call is too long. Bad customer service experiences can leave an especially powerful imprint on women that we will delve into later in the book. The bad news is that if a woman has a terrible experience with your business, she may never forget it. The good news is that if she has a spectacular experience, she'll remember it vividly and tell her friends.

This particular gender difference has several business implications:

- **Sweat the details.**

Never think a woman won't notice something small; she will. Women are thoughtful and appreciate it when businesses are, too. Bank of America has created a "Keep the

Change" marketing program in which it rounds up customer purchases to the nearest dollar and then transfers
the difference from their checking to their savings account. It's a small but thoughtful investment that will
likely pay dividends for Bank of America in customer
loyalty and brand awareness.

- **Ask for feedback.**

When women notice something about your business
that they don't like, prevent them from stewing on it for
weeks, months, and even years by proactively giving
them a chance to provide feedback. It will offer them the
opportunity to vent, and give you a chance to rectify the
problem. Amazon.com and GoDaddy.com, which sells
Internet URL addresses, are two companies that constantly request feedback on their performance by proactively sending surveys and questionnaires. Even when
women don't have time to give it, they appreciate that a
company cared enough to ask.

- **Consider the needs of the other people she's
thinking about.**

Women are constantly thinking about the needs of the
people in their lives, so when you make the lives of those
people better, you earn points with a woman. For instance, if you provide some entertainment for her children while she's shopping, she will be eternally grateful;
if you provide a seat for her husband while she's trying
on clothes, she will be relieved; if she's brought her CEO
along with her on a sales call and you make her look like a
star by complimenting her performance, she will never
forget it.

GENDER DIFFERENCE #5

Women avoid conflict situations. Men avoid emotional scenes.

Why is it that my husband still fast-forwards through the romantic scenes in movies ("Boring," he'll say), while I fast-forward through the blood-and-guts scenes in action films? Scientists contend that women's aversion to conflict has roots in stone-age brain circuitry. In our iPod-wielding, music-downloading, Google-icious world, it's hard to remember that our bodies are still the ancient machines they were back when we lived in caves. The human body and brain are designed for survival of the species, plain and simple.

Brain researcher Louann Brizendine, M.D., argues that women's brains are programmed for social harmony because the survival of the species once depended on it.[23] Back in the wild, if a woman lost her male protector/provider, she and her children would be vulnerable to predators and starvation. It wasn't easy for women to survive on their own and run out of harm's way while toting a gaggle of kids. Consequently, the cavewoman's goal was to keep peace and harmony with other members of the clan to ensure her protection, and to see that her kids made it to adulthood, to continue the circle of life.

Conflict, the theory goes, is thus a traumatic event for women, because on a deep level it may feel like a life-or-death issue. These feelings of aversion are brought on by changes in brain neurochemicals that can be triggered by conflict. The changes are described as an "unbearable" activation of the brain by serotonin, dopamine, and norepinephrine.[24] Tears, nausea, and the feeling of a pit in the stomach are frequent outcomes.

The stone-age survival theory goes hand in hand with anthropologists' ideas about why female friendships are important to women. Women turn to their girlfriends in times of conflict and trouble. If our stone-age gal lost her man during a hunt, she would depend on her girlfriends to help take care of herself and her children, and to ask their male partners to share their food. For women, preserving relationships was long a matter of life and death, and that's why sustaining these friendships is still one of women's greatest needs.

Which means that ads and sales training seminars that use "andro-verbs" such as *annihilate, destroy, crush, nuke,* and *exterminate* simply turn off most women, who are programmed to keep things harmonious and peaceful with the people around them. What's just as bad as violent copy is the increasing use of violent images of women in fashion and liquor advertising, as in the infamous Dolce & Gabbana (D&G) magazine ad that featured a woman who looked like she was about to be raped by a bunch of fabulous-looking but threatening men. When the ad first appeared in late February 2007, the Spanish government was the first to demand its removal. By early March, thirteen Italian senators, both women and men, had joined in protest.[25] D&G complied by withdrawing the ad from circulation in both countries. Morality issues aside, a violent image is just not the kind of motivation that makes a girl want to run out and buy a new blouse.

This gender difference has business implications for marketing in particular. In-your-face campaigns, slogans, and images that glamorize violence, one-upmanship, battles, death, and superiority over lesser mortals are turn-offs to most women.

- **Avoid violent images and language when selling to women.**

Marketing *Terminator*-style will turn off far more women than it attracts. As the keepers of social harmony, women don't view the world as a place full of potential enemies, mutants, and evil combatants. According to Daniel Amen, M.D., the clinical neuroscientist and brain-imaging expert, men have lower activity in the front part of their brains, and need excitement and stimulation if they are to pay attention to something like a marketing message. Which means that violent techniques probably work fairly well with a male audience. Women, on the other hand, have better attention spans but need to have their *emotional* brain stimulated if they are to pay maximum attention. In a Marketing to Moms Coalition study of the best way to relate to mothers in advertising, for example, respondents ranked the following as the best techniques:

1. Depict a woman having fun with her kids.
2. Show her multitasking.
3. Make her laugh.[26]

- **Emphasize positive qualities without being overly negative about your competitors.**

In business, women are turned off by displays of ego and superiority. Try to take the high road whenever you're positioning your business against someone else's. The campaign from Apple, which juxtaposes a laid-back, artsy Mac dude versus a PC geek in a suit, is a gentle example of going head-to-head with a big competitor in a way that's not vicious—although one could argue that it's been viciously effective.

Conversely, as this book is being written, the soup brands Campbell's and Progresso are locked in a heated, nasty battle that the media have dubbed the "Soup Wars" and that seems thousands of miles away from the warm and fuzzy image soup is supposed to engender. Each brand is hurling "bad ingredient" accusations at the other to such a degree that they're being lampooned on shows like *The Colbert Report*. The ads are so similar in looks, tone, and language that it's hard to tell which ones are for Campbell's and which ones are for Progresso. I predict the soup slinging is going to leave a sour taste in the mouths of millions of consumers for both brands, since it has been executed without humor, in a style that feels very tit-for-tat—so much so that one can imagine the executives lying awake at night thinking of new insults to hurl at the other in the next ad. Somehow the fight seems personal, and not about all those people buying the soup.

The Argument for Focusing on the Female Consumer

CLEARLY, gender differences play an important role in how one interprets the world. Recognizing how these differences impact purchasing decisions is a significant first step toward getting in tune with your customers' "female frequency." Here is a summary sheet to help guide you along the way.

How Men and Women View the World Differently

INSIDE WOMEN'S MINDS	INSIDE MEN'S MINDS
Desire to be indispensable.	Desire to be independent.
Desire to be connected.	Desire to be respected.
Wish to minimize status differences.	Awareness of rank in the pack.
Disclose feelings and vulnerabilities.	Hide vulnerabilities. Do not discuss feelings.
Connect with other people by talking.	Connect with other people through activities or by talking about business, politics, or sports.
Feel powerful when they can help others.	Feel powerful when they're in charge of others.
Details about people are the best part of any conversation. There can never be enough detail.	Yawn. Details about people are boring. Technical and sports-related details—now *those* are what's interesting.
Conflict can be stressful.	Conflict is great; it gets the blood going.
Collaboration is more fun.	Collaboration is exciting only if there's a goal to win and someone to beat.
Self-esteem is derived from the quality of relationships in their lives. Achievement is based on internal goals.	Self-esteem is derived from achieving things independently, without help or handouts from others.
What a product does for me is what's most interesting.	How a product works is most interesting.

3

THE FIVE GLOBAL
TRENDS DRIVING
FEMALE CONSUMERS

Like a lot of people in business, I learn about new trends all the time. Since I subscribe to trend-spotting services and newsletters, I'd estimate that I'm exposed to between 10 and 20 new trends each month, which adds up to about 120 to 240 new trends a year. These numbers don't even count all the trends I read about routinely in newspapers and trade magazines. When those are added in, the number probably gets closer to 300 new trends a year—more than one for every workday on the calendar. As much as I enjoy feeling like my fingers are on the pulse, sometimes it feels like sheer trend overload.

I'm not the only one. Many of my colleagues and clients also suffer from trend fatigue. Clearly, no one can or should develop strategies around all the trends we're exposed to on a daily basis. Yet it's easy to see why there's such a big appetite for them—trend data give us what we hope is a useful glimpse into the future, and trends spark our imaginations with their clever names (*greenwashing,* anyone?). But the sheer number of trends being reported on a continuing basis means that there is no possible way to follow all of them. How do we know which ones are meaningful and which aren't? There's the rub.

When it comes to women, it can be more effective to look at the biggest picture of all—the broad demographic changes reflecting the way they are living and working in our specific moment in history. In the case of women, there are five important global demographic changes—five "high hard ones," in corporate-speak—that impact the way women now make purchasing decisions. They are:

1. **The presence of more women in the workforce changes everything.**

   Women's share of the labor force has increased in almost all regions of the world.[1] You already know there are millions of women earning an income. What's less known is how the simple fact of taking a job changes every aspect of a woman's reality—especially how she spends her time and money.

2. **Delayed marriage means more money spent on "me."**

   Women are staying single longer and have more of their own disposable income than ever before. These young women have yet to be targeted or even recognized seriously by industries outside of luxury goods, apparel, and cosmetics, even though they earn substantial paychecks.

3. **Lower birthrates globally mean fewer kids but more "stuff."**

   When it comes to fertility rates, the numbers are down, particularly in industrialized countries. Unsurprisingly, people's decision to have fewer kids has major implications for consumer spending patterns. But if you're guessing that spending on kids is down, guess again.

4. **The divorce economy means two of everything.**

   Nearly half of all American marriages end in divorce, and divorce rates have increased across the world.[2] While the societal effects of broken marriages have been studied in great detail, the effects of divorce on the consumer economy have been underreported. The reality of divorce is that it unleashes a torrent of consumer spending—and not just on divorce lawyers.

5. **The presence of more older women redefines target markets.**

   Look at enough advertising briefs and you might think that everyone older than fifty-four is dead, or at the very least broke. But that couldn't be further from the truth. The older population has been steadily increasing its numbers and will continue to do so for decades. By 2050, for the first time in human history, the global elderly will outnumber children.[3] The opportunities are as enormous as the population itself.

That's the big picture. Now let's get more specific about what this might mean to your business.

The Feminization of the Workforce

The global economic downturn has had countless implications, but one of the most notable is that women are now poised to overtake men in the American workforce for the first time in history.[4] The bread-winning woman has forever changed the face of the global economy.

From Canada to China (where most women have worked since the time of Mao), from Japan to Mexico, women's participation in the workforce is impacting the way they spend money and how they make purchasing decisions. In nearly all developing countries, the proportion of working women in informal employment is greater than the proportion of working men.[5]

The advent of working women has not only increased household income (particularly in industrialized countries), it's significantly changed consumer spending patterns along the way. Seventy percent of American women with kids under eighteen are earning a paycheck while raising their children.[6] *Seventy percent.* That's a lot of working moms, with needs and wants that are different because of the inherent tension involved in managing both a family and a career.

The shift of women to working outside the home has been under way for nearly forty years, and there's no turning back. From a consumer standpoint, every time a woman takes a job outside the home, her spending patterns are altered. Not only does she increase her household income, she wears different clothes, eats different foods, travels in a different direction on the roadways, involves other people in caring for her children if she has them, and has a different relationship with money. If it's a job she likes, she may even look at herself differently, with increased confidence. In short, an outside job impacts:

- When she shops
- Where she shops
- What she buys
- What car she drives
- When she eats
- What she eats
- What she wears
- Where she lives
- How much she is prepared to spend on any given product or service
- How much money she invests and where she banks
- How she uses health care providers and insurance programs
- Where, when, and how long she goes on vacation

And then there's the multiplication effect: every time a woman heads off to a job, the event changes not only her own life but also the lives of everyone around her. This is especially true if she has a family. Her participation in the workforce impacts:

- What her family eats
- When her family eats
- Where her children go during the day
- How many "helpers" are employed in the household—from babysitters to housecleaners and tutors

- When she schedules her kids' appointments
- Where her family lives
- What her husband's family responsibilities are, if she's married
- How much time she and her kids spend in the car
- How and where her family spends its leisure time

"When a mother goes off to work, the whole family hustles differently. It creates a domino effect that impacts everyone in the household," says Eric Elder, a senior executive for Ryland Homes, one of America's largest home builders. Ryland has redesigned a number of the floor plans of its homes around the phenomenon of working women and their families. The company has discovered that not only does working change a woman's personal traffic patterns, it also changes the needs of her physical environment. We'll examine exactly what Ryland has done to accommodate these changes in the next chapter.

When Women Work, Economies Grow

WOMEN have worked since the beginning of time, but since their efforts historically were confined to the unpaid environment of the home, their contributions had less impact on factors that drive economic growth. Not anymore. Women are the engine of the global economy. As the *Economist* magazine trumpeted in a widely publicized article, "Forget China, India and the Internet: economic growth is driven by women."[7] And since service jobs continue to replace those in the manufacturing sector, the opportunities for women have never been greater. Not many jobs require big muscles anymore. With so many women working outside the home these days, we not only understand their economic power, we also have a better sense of the economic contribution of stay-at-home moms, since there is now widespread awareness that quality child care is expensive, and comes with its own set of management issues.

In the United States, the growth rate of women in the labor force has been much faster than men's for the last twenty years. Women have filled two new jobs for every one taken by a man since 1970.[8] And according to predictions made by the U.S. Bureau of Labor Statistics, women's job growth will still be slightly higher than men's until at least the year 2014.[9] After three decades of growth in workforce participation, one-quarter of all married women now earn more money than their husbands.[10] This is a far cry from the 1960s, when married women couldn't get credit cards or mortgages in their own names, and female employees could be fired just for getting pregnant or old.

Recessions notwithstanding, the size of the labor force gender gap is a good way to measure a country's economic health. It's no coincidence that Scandinavian countries, with their high levels of women in the workforce, are considered to have the highest standards of living in the world. Urban women in emerging economies such as Brazil, China, and India are altering the consumer landscape with their paychecks. Conversely, the lack of women's participation in many Middle Eastern economies is one of the factors holding these countries back. They have yet to unleash the energy and intellectual contributions of half of their population.

More Paychecks Equal More Disposable Income

ONE of Goldman Sachs' finest minds on the subject, Kevin Daly, has a compelling analysis:

> As the male-female employment gap closes, female disposable income growth will surpass male income growth . . . the relative rise in female affluence is also likely to result in a shift in consumption patterns; a shift that is likely to be most notable as female incomes exceed the level required to acquire essential goods and services, and rise to the point where a significant proportion of income can be spent on discretionary goods.[11]

In other words, working women don't just earn money, they spend it. Based on the labor force data, women are now (and will continue to be for the foreseeable future), the bull's-eye for consumer goods manufacturers. This is a particularly valuable insight for multinational companies trying to penetrate and grow in emerging markets. Studying the female labor-force participation trends in countries such as Brazil, Russia, India, and China can help provide a road map to how women's daily lives are changing and what it means in terms of economic opportunity for your business.

The Working Mother: Do You Know Her?

WORKING moms are everywhere, and yet the reality of their lives is unknown to many of the colleagues who toil alongside them. This is because, generally speaking, women try to make the work-life balance look easy (which it isn't) and don't want to be viewed as less committed at work by talking at length about family responsibilities. The situation is different for their male colleagues. When men have children, it often enhances their status at work. They're viewed as being more committed to the job because they have a family depending on their paycheck. Marriage and children make a man appear stable and responsible; this usually helps him get ahead. Even today, it's hard to run for a major political office or to make it as a CEO of a big company as a single man.

When women have children, it can have the opposite effect. The perception at work is that a woman's family responsibilities will be a distraction. Employers know that a woman may need time off when her child gets sick or when she has babysitting issues. In many countries, it's assumed that a woman's working life is over with her first pregnancy. Though some companies are genuinely working hard to create more family-friendly and female-friendly work environments, women are still aware that motherhood isn't considered an asset in most careers. They're also conscious that child-related absences may create additional work for their colleagues, which is just one reason that the tension between family and career can be stressful.

When men take time off work to do something with their children, they're often seen as noble, because they're pitching in with parenthood and being good dads. Women do not receive the same reflected glory. A midlevel executive named Melanie told me this story:

One of our big bosses at work has a sick wife. He told us last week that she has stage IV cancer and not much longer to live. He has two young kids. This is a tragic situation, but I couldn't help but notice the reaction he's gotten from all the men in the office. They're all standing in doorways whispering, "How is Mike going to handle the kids? How is he going to get them to school and pick them up, take care of them when they're sick, and still do his job?" And so on and so on.

The ironic part is that these conversations are taking place in the hallways, where all of us women can hear them. Most of us are mothers, and quite a few of us are single mothers, and we all handle these very situations every day of our lives. But the men can't see it, because they've never had to do it on their own, and we don't complain about it. So when it comes to talking about Mike's situation, we just shake our heads in sympathy and say nothing about the fact that Mike is simply going to be doing what half the women in the office do already.

The double standard still exists because modern corporate culture was built in the years following World War II, and created on a model in which male executives were expected to have a wife at home to take care of every aspect of their personal lives. What makes it difficult for women—and for all parents—is that no matter how much the workplace changes, there is no getting around the simple fact that young children cannot stay home alone all day and raise themselves. Somebody's got to do it.

"What I Need Is a Wife"

YOU'LL often hear working women say, "What I need is a wife." It's shorthand for "I need someone to take care of all the endless errands and housekeeping, so I have more time to focus on what's important." We're going to dissect this big trend of working women by analyzing an average day in the life of just one. We'll call her Jamie, and even though Jamie earns a good salary in a white-collar job in Chicago, her family's life is stretched to the breaking point by child care costs and the juggling act that comes from all four members of the family going in different directions every morning. She is like many of your customers.

Do you know her?
A typical day in the life of an everywoman

Name: .... Jamie
Age: 40
Job: .... Manager at commercial real estate firm
Family: .... Husband, two kids
Pets: .... One goldfish
Location: ...... Chicago

MORNING

5:15:   Wakes up, showers, gets dressed.

6:00:   Wakes up kids.

6:30:   Feeds and dresses kids and prepares their food and snacks for the day.

7:00:   Leaves house, straps kids in car seats.

7:15:   Drops off one child at preschool.

7:30:   Drops off other child at day care center.

7:45:   Parks car in corporate parking garage.

8:00:   Stops at Dunkin' Donuts for large coffee.

8:15:   Arrives at desk and eats yogurt while checking e-mail.

8:30:   Officially starts the day.

AFTERNOON

12:00:   Eats lunch at desk and does as many family errands as possible by phone and e-mail (pays bills online, books appointments online, calls the pediatrician).

1:00:   Back to work.

4:00:   Checks in with babysitter to see if she has safely picked up Jamie's older child from preschool.

5:45:   Leaves work and picks up her younger child at day care.

EVENING

6:00:   Drives home thinking about dinner. She's too tired to make something but her stomach is growling. Maybe she'll have something delivered? She calls her husband to see if he has any ideas. He doesn't. "Let's just scrounge," she says into the phone.

6:30:   Dismisses the babysitter and feeds kids the minute she gets home; she doesn't even change out of her work clothes. Her husband isn't home yet because he has a longer commute.

7:00:   Husband gets home and they decide whose turn it is to bathe the kids, then put them in pajamas.

7:30:   Jamie and her husband look through the kitchen cabinets for something to eat. They each choose something different, and both meals involve the microwave as the only cooking instrument. They eat while they play with their kids.

8:00:   Husband starts the process of putting the younger child to bed.

8:30:   Jamie starts the process of putting the older child to bed.

9:00:   Both kids are asleep.

9:15:   Jamie and her husband turn on the TV to find something they both like. Each of them uses their laptop while watching TV. Jamie looks at her e-mail to see if anything new has happened since she left the office. She answers some messages and starts thinking about the day ahead. Has some fun reading news, personal e-mails, and celebrity gossip online. Starts to relax.

9:45:   After thirty minutes, Jamie feels like she's relaxed long enough. She puts the dishes away and checks the laundry to make sure everyone has clean clothes for tomorrow. She picks up the living room and looks at the mail.

10:45: After watching a recorded show from their DVR, Jamie and her husband set the alarm for 5:15. Before she goes to sleep, Jamie spends fifteen minutes looking at women's magazines in bed. As she flips the pages, she imagines herself in all the beautiful clothes, shoes, and homes, and dreams of being as thin and gorgeous as the smiling celebrities. She looks at the beauty tips and makes mental notes for the next time she's out shopping. Maybe she

should change her hair color. Maybe Target
will have some good, cheap knock-offs of the
expensive styles in the magazine. Maybe she
should get some flats—looks like they're in
this season.

To Jamie, her stash of magazines is the perfect way to wind down at the end of the day with some harmless fun, and she considers them a little reward for working so hard. Her husband makes fun of her *Us Weekly* subscription, but she doesn't care. It's only about $50 a year, and to her it's worth every penny, because it and the other women's magazines on her nightstand are her harmless guilty pleasure. They also keep her in touch with what other people are talking about around the euphemistic "water cooler" at work. Like countless women around the world, Jamie dozes off thinking about new clothes, a fitter body, a more glamorous self, and all the things she has to accomplish tomorrow. She sums up her life this way:

> *I feel like I've had a full day of work before I even get to work. As a working mom, I almost feel like an athlete in training. During the Olympics, the reporters always talk about how the athletes trained every day for ten years starting at four o'clock in the morning, and everyone wonders how they did it. That's the best analogy I can think of for what it feels like to be a working mom. I'm like a professional athlete, just without the perfect body.*

Is Jamie an extreme example of a working mom? No. A day like Jamie's is reality for millions of women, the majority of whom still carry the burden of household responsi-

bilities when they're off the clock of their day jobs, in a phenomenon known as the "second shift." For single working
mothers and those earning lower salaries than Jamie, the
days are even harder. These women tend to rely on family
members for child care and have very little time and money
left over each month to spend on themselves.

Stay-at-home moms are often just as busy. The term itself is a misnomer, since most of these women are out and
about all day, working hard on behalf of their families. In
fact, many women who identify themselves as stay-at-home
moms are actually engaged in some kind of outside labor
activity—whether it's freelancing, selling products in the
direct-sales industry, or volunteering—in addition to their
career managing their families. Many lead lives that are
just as busy and complicated as those who work outside
the home.

Imagine that your customer is Jamie, or any other busy
working woman. How could your company help her? Consider the following:

- **Working women need services, not just products.**
  In the era of working women, customer service could be
  your most compelling advantage. It all comes down to
  that little four-letter word: *help*.

  No matter what your business, there's room to improve
  your customer service. What can you do to ensure that
  your product or service helps women in a way that goes
  beyond their expectations? How can you maximize their
  productivity and make them feel smarter just for choosing you? A few weeks ago I walked into a shoe store in
  Berkeley, California, that had a pedicure station in it. For
  a store in a climate where lots of people wear open-toed

shoes, it's a simple example of a *why-hasn't-anyone-thought-of-this-before* service that complements a product offering. What broader context of your own product or service can you leverage to create a complementary service? What company or other brand could you partner with that you haven't already?

• **Working women need extended hours and more delivery options.**

Every morning on her way to work, Jamie passes an Ann Taylor shop that doesn't open until ten a.m. She says she often finds herself looking longingly in the windows, knowing there's not a snowball's chance in hell that she'll be able to get there once the workday begins. However, if the store opened a few hours earlier, she might just find the time to go. Extended hours can provide busy women the incentive they need to stop what they're doing during the day and pay attention to your brand. Whatever you can do to make Jamie's life easier, especially during the week, can help you stay ahead of your competitors, who may use only weekend-specific campaigns and promotions.

Delivery options in all kinds of categories can find a receptive audience with busy women. The Sleep Squad is a Chicago-based mattress retailer that shows up at customers' homes with a mobile mattress showroom in a specially designed truck. Customers can take a "test rest" on the mattresses, and if they like one, the Sleep Squad will install it in their home on the spot and take away the old mattress at no charge. What a stress-free way to shop for a new bed, without the awkwardness of having to lay down on mattresses in a busy, public shop.

- **Cars are second homes to many working women.**

Working women in North America, and in particular those who are mothers of young kids, spend an inordinate amount of time in their cars.

Casual service restaurants, such as Outback Steakhouse, have recognized the stuck-in-the-car phenomenon and revitalized their weeknight offerings through curbside take-out services, where customers can take a hot meal home without ever getting out of the car and without feeling like they've resorted to fast food. Snack brands, from gums to candies and crackers, now offer packaging in round shapes that fit into a car's cup holders for easy grabbing while behind the wheel. In-car DVD players have become a godsend for family road trips. In a nutshell, the car has become like a second home. Whether it's audio books from business-to-business companies or mini refrigerators from home appliance manufacturers, it's worth considering how to adapt your own product or service to the environment of the car.

It still shocks me that FM radio, that mainstay of automobile entertainment, offers so little in terms of women's programming. Women dominate viewership of morning breakfast shows on television, but where is radio? It's strange that talk radio is almost exclusively the domain of men, when it's actually women who are society's biggest talkers and who spend so much time in their cars running errands and shuttling kids around. It can sometimes seem as if the terrestrial radio industry is not paying attention to half the market, when it should be using every tool in its arsenal to compete with iPods and satellite radio. Even in an age when everyone is chasing digital media, radio remains a wide-open frontier for advertisers to get creative and come up with programming that has female appeal.

- **Errand running and shopping compression occur on weekends, with the kids if she has any.**

Because they're often too busy to shop during the week, working women save their big shopping excursions for the weekends, which is precisely when the stores are crowded with everyone else. Because school's out and the babysitter's off, weekend shopping warriors tend to be with their kids. Naturally, the kids' presence completely transforms any kind of retail outing, and not necessarily in ways that make things easier.

Look at what happened when Jamie tried to buy a car with her husband.

We decided to buy a new car because we had a second child and needed something bigger. So we went to the Mazda dealership, where we had to bring our children and our car seats. When you're a family, you have to bring your children with you to make sure they fit in the car, especially where car seats are involved. Not only did the dealership have nothing aesthetically pleasing in their sales area—just desks and chairs—you couldn't even get water. There was one broken vending machine. I had a two-and-a-half-year-old and a four-year-old with me. The car-buying experience for anyone seems to be at least a three-hour process from start to finish. It was excruciating for us as a family, because our youngest child was going crazy. The only thing to play with inside the sales area were the new cars. The outside area was dangerous because it was a parking lot filled with moving cars.

We eventually ran out of food, water, and toys. (We didn't expect it to take three hours.) I actually had to leave my husband there to complete the transaction, and then I had to pack up the kids in the car again and go pick him up two hours later. It was a nightmare experience for us. It was clear that there was not an ounce of thought given to families. They had nothing for children. Even a balloon would have bought us a half hour. Yet I would guess that 80 percent of the cars on the lot were for families—SUVs, minivans, et cetera. It wasn't like we were at a Porsche dealership. Because I had to leave the transaction early, I don't even have my own name on the title—just my husband's, which is ironic because I'm the primary breadwinner. It was shocking. All they needed was a kids' play area. It's such fierce competition in the car business, it's like all you need to do is offer a pleasant experience and you can get the families. Why don't they know this?

Being kid friendly can offer a major competitive advantage. Kid factors can be taken into consideration for everything from how wide the parking spots are (wide enough to get strollers out the side door of a minivan?) to what kind of entertainment is on offer for them once inside an establishment.

There are lots of other complications to shopping on weekends, and not just the obvious ones such as fighting the crowds. For one thing, research shows that working mothers like Jamie often do their big weekly grocery shopping on Sunday afternoons, which is a bad day of the week to buy fresh foods, since there are typically few store deliveries that day.[12] It's easy to see why online shopping has such huge appeal for working women.

In many ways, traditional businesses have yet to catch up to the activity patterns of working women. This means there's an opportunity to create all kinds of helpful offerings to accommodate their time and convenience issues.

- **Working women develop a sense of humor as a coping mechanism.**

Jamie uses humor to deal with her stress, but most marketers shy away from being funny with women. This is certainly not true with men's brands, such as Anheuser-Busch and Old Spice, just to give two examples, which produce very funny ads to great effect. Thus far there has been no female equivalent of anything like Budweiser's famous "Wassssup!" advertising campaign. As Jamie likes to say, "No one could use a good laugh more than a working mom." So why do so few companies offer her one? Humorous portrayals of life in all its messy glory are a powerful and underused tool for connecting with women, especially mothers.

Suave is one brand that's used a humor-based campaign successfully. Working with the lighthearted theme "Motherhood isn't always pretty," the hair care brand's marketers, in conjunction with telecommunications giant Sprint, created an "In the Motherhood" online community that featured stories inspired by real mothers (who submitted them to the website) acted out in short video "webisodes" by actresses Leah Remini, Jenny McCarthy, and Chelsea Handler. Women found the tone funny, authentic, and fun, and the webisodes were viewed more than twenty million times. In a kind of reverse leap of marketing, the webisodes were developed into a (short-lived) network television show by American broadcaster ABC.[13]

GLOBAL TREND #2

Delayed Marriage Means More Money Spent on "Me"

"I do" is starting to turn into "I will—someday." All over the industrialized world, women are getting married later in life. Back in 1965, the age of first marriage for an American woman was just twenty. Forty years later, the age of first marriage has crept up to twenty-five.[14] In Western European countries such as France and the Netherlands, the average age is thirty, and cohabitation in lieu of marriage is common and socially acceptable. The situation is similar in Sweden, where the age of first marriage for a woman is an astonishing (from an American point of view) thirty-two years old.

In addition to the social acceptability of living together, higher education is a big driver of this trend. Female college graduates are taking their degrees and putting them to good use in their postcollegiate years. Young women in several American cities including New York, Dallas, Chicago, and Los Angeles are making more money than their male counterparts, which has resulted in all kinds of interesting new wrinkles in the relations between the sexes, especially for dating couples.[15] It's a new situation for young women, in which their mothers cannot usually provide much advice.

From homes to fine furniture, single women are no longer waiting to buy all the things that used to be expected of their future Prince Charmings. They buy cars. Diamonds.

Vacations. Mutual funds. Power tools. And more than ever, they're buying homes. Single women are the fastest-growing demographic in the U.S. real estate market. As noted in Chapter 1, they now buy 20 percent of all homes.[16]

All over the world, young urban women are driving trends in luxury, fashion, and design, and brands as established as Lincoln Mercury are starting to employ young women to design their cars of the future.

The trend shows no sign of abating. Women earn the majority of bachelor's and associate's degrees in the United States and have done so for almost twenty years.[17] It's not just an American phenomenon; in most developed countries, more women than men go to university.[18] In the United States, women earn 57 percent of bachelor's degrees and 59 percent of master's degrees, and they account for 51 percent of students enrolled in medical school, as well as nearly half of those enrolled in law school.[19] This is the primary reason that women's spending power and workforce participation are predicted to increase for the next several decades. Better education amounts to better jobs, better pay, and better financial security.

After earning their degrees, women often spend the next several years single while they establish their careers. It's during this time of life that they start spending serious money on themselves.

It's surprising how many industries underestimate the buying power of young women. Too many salespeople haven't accepted the idea that single women can and do buy big-ticket items such as cars and houses, so they often don't take this sales opportunity seriously. Or, worse, they try to take advantage of what seems like a vulnerability. Single women still feel they must resort to the age-old trick of bringing a male friend or relative along with them for high-cost purchases, to guard against being taken advantage of. This extra effort and inconvenience ensure that sales are regularly being lost. Industries ranging from luxury goods to automobiles to housing must get wise to the power of the young female consumer. Not only should she be taken seriously, she should be catered to seriously. Just because she's wearing a ponytail doesn't mean she's not earning a big, fat paycheck.

Stereotypes are slow to die. It seems there's never a news story about single women without an accompanying photo of Carrie Bradshaw, the character on *Sex and the City* played by Sarah Jessica Parker. Carrie's character became the Mary Tyler Moore for the millennium: the poster girl for the modern single female. Emotionally, the Carrie character struck a major chord with women around the world. But from a consumer-spending standpoint, Carrie Bradshaw was all hat and no cattle. In the show, Carrie only bought expensive shoes, cocktails, and accessories that no real Manhattan-based freelance writer could ever afford. Real single women are making a much bigger impact.

What insights can you take from these data?

- **Young women buy big-ticket items and business-to-business services.**
What's needed is coaching for salespeople to treat them seriously and to speak to these women in a way that connects with them. As one twenty-two-year-old working woman recounted to me, "When I called Firestone to check on my car, the guy at the other end of the line asked if I could put my dad on the phone so he could explain what was wrong—even though the car is mine, and my

dad lives fifteen hundred miles away and has nothing to do with it."

Hiring more women as salespeople would help solve part of the problem. For instance, only about 10 percent of all automotive sales representatives are women, which doesn't remotely reflect the diversity of the automotive customer base, and has the added side effect of making you feel like you have to set your watch back to 1972 when you step into a dealership.

- **Young single women are high-frequency entertainment consumers.**

Wherever you can find a chilled chardonnay or a fruity drink, look for the women out in packs, having a laugh and talking about every detail of their lives.

There's a huge opportunity for the development of "girlfriend" packages across a variety of industries, most of which still cater to traditional couples and families. Travel is the hottest example. "Girlfriend getaways" are the biggest thing going, and they've spawned both a magazine and a website of the same name. A study from the American Automobile Association shows that 24 percent of American women have taken a girlfriend getaway with female family and friends in the past three years, and 39 percent of American women plan on taking one in the next three years. This has massive implications for girlfriend packages at restaurants, hotels, retail stores, cultural activities, educational classes, and gyms—basically, everywhere that women go.

Young women can and do spend money on their friends, in the form of birthday parties, gifts, bachelorette parties, bridal showers, cocktails, food, and celebrations of every stripe. If you can find an easy way to package your product or service as a gift, you may very well find a whole new audience. The ladies need to buy their presents somewhere, and maybe you can help them do it.

- **Women celebrate "girl power" and a new kind of femininity.**

Empowering "girl power" brands aren't just for kids and preteens anymore. Companies such as Benefit, a cosmetics brand run by two sisters who clearly have a sense of humor, feature products with names like Some Kinda Gorgeous, Dear John, Honey . . . Snap Out of It!, Bad Gal Blue, and Miss Popularity. Young women are drawn to Benefit's kitschy, retro, girly messages. It's empowerment sold with a wink, as personified by Reese Witherspoon's character, Elle Woods, in the movie *Legally Blonde*. These gals may be carrying a pink Hello Kitty bag, but they're doing it in an ironic way . . . because hey, they're in law school!

- **Women notice when companies talk to them.**

Changing perceptions of categories that were once the domain of couples is important. The much-heralded campaign promoting diamond rings for the right hand is one of the best examples of how to sell luxury with an empowerment message. The Diamond Trading company, a part of De Beers, famously created a marketing campaign that told women they didn't need a man to deserve a diamond, and that they should buy one for their right hand. It was a strategy as brilliant as a shiny, two-carat rock.

Citibank also gets kudos for its clever "Women and Company" campaigns, which appeal to a female target audience with messages such as "Small loans for big girls." Citibank effectively juxtaposes witty language with a serious message.

GLOBAL TREND #3

Lower Birthrates Mean Fewer Kids but More "Stuff"

Ah, to be a kid again . . . *just to get all that stuff!*

Even though birthrates have gone down all over the industrialized world, as well as in many developing countries, parents spend money on kids and babies like never before. The U.S. market for juvenile products is about $9 billion annually, which is more than double the figure from 1995.[20] Kids are on the receiving end of more goodies than people ever could have imagined fifty years ago. Yet take a look at the size of the shrinking American household over the years:

> 1915 . . . . 4.5 people
> 1967 . . . . 3.3 people
> 2006 . . . . 2.6 people[21]

It's ironic that in America we're living in much bigger homes crammed with so much more stuff—and rental storage units for the overflow—and yet so many fewer people. It will be interesting to see if the lingering effects of the bad economy include a return to smaller spaces, with the accompanying smaller mortgages.

For most adults, kids have become a lifestyle choice. According to the U.S. Census, nearly half of all women of childbearing age—44 percent—have no children.[22] The percentage of American women having only one child has more than doubled in twenty years, to almost one-quarter. And while U.S. Census data show that we might be at the beginning of an upswing in the number of kids people are choosing to have (in 2006 the nation's total fertility rate was above replacement levels for the first time since 1971), the average American woman is still predicted to have two kids in her lifetime. This is a relatively high number when compared to the rest of the developed world. Japan (1.2 kids per woman) and Italy (1.3 per woman) are two of the countries with the lowest birthrates, and their governments are scrambling to find ways to reverse the trend. Even countries with historically large families are seeing lowering fertility rates. Mexico, for instance, has a fertility rate of 2.3 children per woman.[23]

There are as many reasons for small families as there are parents. Some women get married so late in life they find they can't have many biological children; others decide that having just one means their child will have the best of everything; and still others believe that having a singleton is the only way they can manage both work and family life well. And then, of course, there are many women and men who simply prefer not to have children because they enjoy the freedom childlessness offers. We are lucky to have a choice; in China, the one-child policy created in 1979 still stands, though it's often waived for many people in rural areas and ignored by those who have enough money to pay the fines instead.

Across the world, parents are lavishing more time, attention, and money on their precious few children. From the phenomenon of the "little emperors" in China—the moniker for indulged only children—to American tots cruising around in $850 Bugaboo strollers, middle- and upper-class babies have never had it better. And not only do today's children get more stuff, they have a fundamentally different relationship with their parents, benefiting from the time, attention, and opportunities that a child who is one of six can't command.

Whether it's your local Starbucks, fine restaurants, boutiques, and even bars—parents bring their kids *everywhere*. And when their kids get older, many parents are so involved in their children's lives that some schools are forced to adopt policies that limit the amount of time they can spend in their child's classrooms. By having fewer children, parents put all their eggs in fewer baskets, and they're determined to make sure they hatch with every possible advantage.

The modern appetite to lavish children with the best that money can buy is creating entirely new industries. From high-end children's party-planning companies to the entire spectrum of designer baby products, such as Kate Spade diaper bags and Baby Dior dresses, the global economy is benefiting from an exciting new customer base who used to be clad in nothing more than cloth diapers, Garanimals, and Sears Toughskins.

What insights can your business take from these data?

- **Mothers are older, wealthier, and more educated than at any other time in history.**
It's no longer uncommon to see well-dressed parents in their mid-forties at preschool events. Schools are demanding, and getting, parental involvement on a scale unthinkable back in the old days (when, ironically, parents may have had more free time to get involved).

Many educated women are dropping out of their executive posts and entering "pro-tirement," a clever new word that means they are leaving their corporate jobs earlier than expected, for new careers managing their families' lives. These MBA-, JD-, and even MD-wielding mommies are bringing their Fortune 500 negotiating skills to kindergartens, playgrounds, and PTA meetings across the country, and changing the tone of school and community relationships in affluent areas.

From Gymboree to Leapfrog, businesses promoting products that give children an educational advantage find a receptive audience with these women. And because moms spend a lot of energy organizing their kids' activities, software and electronic gadgets that are sold with messages about staying connected to their kids find an interested audience with modern moms.

- **Savvy kids impact their parents' purchasing decisions more than ever.**

Kids' opinions are weighed heavily in family purchasing decisions, especially those involving technology. When the Internet connection isn't working, everyone knows to ask the twelve-year-old to fix it. Unsurprisingly, single mothers tend to involve their children in product decisions and technology issues more than women with husbands.

Because kids are on the receiving end of so many commercial messages, they become brand conscious at an early age and, more than ever, influence the brands their parents buy for them. My six-year-old nephew asked for a Darth Vader watch for his birthday, even though he has never seen the original *Star Wars* movie, and wouldn't recognize Harrison Ford or Carrie Fisher if they served him pancakes for breakfast. The *Star Wars* marketing machine rages on after more than thirty years, capturing yet another generation through the branding of toys, dolls, video games, prequels, and sequels. It has successfully capitalized on the nostalgia of parents and grandparents, who are the people shelling out the money for these products.

- **Many kids are being raised with luxuries that were once reserved for adults.**

From two-year-olds traveling with their parents in business-class airline seats (using their working parents' miles) to kids' birthday parties at hotel spas, the standards for kid luxury are climbing higher every year. Gone are pin-the-tail-on-the-donkey games and homemade chocolate cake for birthday parties. Parents sometimes feel pressured to do things such as rent an inflatable moonwalk for the entire neighborhood or take the whole crew to an amusement park. The cost of raising kids is *not* getting cheaper—it's going in the other direction.

Smaller families often travel in nicer family cars. People who grew up riding in wood-paneled Ford Country Squire station wagons—sitting facing backwards in the "way back"—are now driving their kids around in $50,000 Audis, complete with individual DVD players and headphones.

Service businesses that cater to well-heeled children are finding a willing audience in their parents. Specialty hair salons, nail salons, pottery classes, spas, and other kid versions of adult luxuries are growing. Sometimes I find it jarring when I sit down for a pedicure and discover that the client next to me is an eleven-year-old girl. (It wasn't until college that I got my first pedicure.) With fewer kids, parents are often willing to spend adult-sized sums of money on them. And since they've had them later in life, they're bringing the kids into their own adult world far more than previous generations did.

GLOBAL TREND #4

The Divorce Economy

Many of the people reading this book already know about the divorce economy because they've experienced it firsthand.

Though marriage is viewed as a private decision between a man and a woman, divorce has a far-reaching public impact. From the expense of lawyers and the bureaucratic costs of judges, courts, and programs such as child support enforcement and Medicaid, to the increasing number of children flying alone on airplanes for visits to noncustodial parents, the impact on the consumer economy begins with the simple fact that every divorce results in at least one geographic move, and in many cases two. Each divorce causes a torrent of consumer spending, and not just on divorce lawyers. As the character Ricky Bobby's sons, Walker and Texas Ranger, squeal in the movie *Talladega Nights,* "*Divorce? Yeah, two Christmases!*"

Divorce rates are skyrocketing in Japan, soaring in China, and high in Korea, and they've doubled in Italy over the last ten years.[24] They are even on the rise in India, where marriage is the most sacred of cultural institutions. In the United States, the number remains at just under half of all marriages, with divorce being slightly less common among people with college educations.

Women historically have been plunged into a lower standard of living after divorce, as a result of losing their husbands' income and benefits. While this is still true, the picture is improving, driven in part by the fact that so many married women now earn their own paychecks and are gainfully employed at the time of divorce. The result is that for some women, divorce is now a cause for *celebration*—complete with celebratory girlfriend parties. This is a new phenomenon that would have been inconceivable a few decades ago, when being divorced carried a heavy social and moral stigma.

The economic freedom to leave a bad marriage is just one reason that in Western countries, women are the filers in the majority of divorce cases.[25] Another reason is that most mothers feel reasonably confident they'll be awarded primary custody of their children, which isn't necessarily true in many parts of the developing world.

In every part of the globe, divorce is becoming a more common fact of life. There are several contributing factors to this trend:

- More women around the world are gaining an education and earning money, so fewer people (of either sex) are trapped in bad relationships for purely economic reasons.
- In many developing countries, women have made strides in obtaining legal rights as individuals, not just as daughters and wives. They have also been exposed to Western conceptions about romantic love and the idea of self-fulfillment.
- Over the past twenty years, most countries have made it

easier for couples to get divorced. All the traditionally Catholic countries of Latin and South America, for instance, now allow divorce. In 2004, Chile became the last country in the Western Hemisphere to legalize divorce.

- In many cultures where keeping mistresses is common-place, such as the modern Chinese cities of Beijing and Shanghai, women are fighting back and saying to their husbands, "You can't have both me and a mistress; if you want to keep her, then *hasta la vista*." Or as they say in Mandarin Chinese, *zai jian*.

Let's take a peek at the life of a divorced woman who embodies several of the trends in this chapter. We'll call her Katherine, and she is real, but her name has been changed. As you read about her, try to imagine how your product or service could fit into her life.

Katherine was twenty-five when she married Tom, her college boyfriend. Like so many couples, they were a perfect match until they weren't anymore, for reasons neither could articulate well. The couple grew apart. Tom wound up having an affair with someone at work, and Katherine filed for divorce just after the couple's eighth wedding anniversary. The judge allowed Katherine and Tom to share joint custody of their four-year-old son, and they now balance child care duties in an amicable way. They have chosen to live just a few miles apart from each other, to make shared parenting a bit easier.

Katherine has since remarried and had a daughter with her new husband. She works full time, and so does Tom. All the grandparents help with child care and transportation issues, for which Tom and Katherine feel grateful and lucky. The grandparents live nearby and have the resources and inclination to help. Often, Katherine's daughter joins Tom and their son to run errands or participate in birthday parties and other activities that involve mutual friends. Katherine even purchased a second child seat for Tom's car, specifically for her daughter to use when she is with him.

Tom, therefore, often finds himself taking care of a little girl who is not biologically or legally his. For the most part, he's happy to do it, and considers himself her uncle. The way he sees it, the girl is his son's sibling and therefore an important part of his son's life. It's complicated, and there are three sets of grandparents in play at any given time, and the holidays are crazy, but somehow they make it work. There are many sacrifices—Katherine's new husband, for instance, already had to turn down a job offer because of the need for his stepson to have close proximity to Tom. The boy has two bedrooms (one in each home), two sets of clothes, two bikes, two sets of toys, two Sony PlayStation consoles, at least two birthday parties every year, and one Christmas and one Hannukah.

As a working mother who balances a high-profile job, a custody schedule, a new spouse and an old spouse, and children who are in a half-sibling relationship with each other, Katherine is an embodiment of the modern divorced woman.

The New Singlehood

WIDESPREAD divorce has created a new, distinct period of singlehood in many women's lives. This means that millions of women now find themselves single in three distinct phases of life:

1. In their twenties, before they get married
2. In midlife, when nearly half get divorced
3. At the end of life, since women live longer than men

The second stage of singlehood is unique. For one thing, women respond to divorce differently than men. Once the heartache is (theoretically) over, women are often on a mission to completely reinvent themselves, from their appearance to their job to their lifestyle, all with the goal of making a fresh start. After compromising their own tastes and desires in a relationship for so long, it can be a joyful exercise for these women to go out and discover what their own taste is in clothes, furniture, food, cars, and decor. They want to travel, they want to experience things, and they want to taste what they feel they've been missing.

After Divorce, Women Aren't Just the Other Half; They're the Only Half

DIVORCE can be a squeamish subject for businesspeople, but whether we like it or not, the notions of household and family have shifted—perhaps irrevocably. In the United States, the traditional nuclear family is now the minority type of household for the first time in modern history.[26] The positive aspects of this reality should be reflected in the images, marketing messages, and sales language used by any organization.

It's sobering to realize that fully one-third of all American babies are born to unmarried women and that more than a quarter of all households (27 percent) are run by a single woman.[27] Depictions of nuclear families exclusively may seem ideal to many people within a corporation, but they risk alienating divorced and single women—the very women with 100 percent purchasing power for their households. Since many senior-level male executives are married with children, it's important to make sure their own life experiences don't skew the decisions meant for an audience with a different reality.

What are the insights for business?

- **With each divorce comes the need for both people in the marriage to make themselves whole again.**

Messages that tap into women's constant desire for reinvention are particularly powerful at this time of life. Events like divorce showers and "relaunch" parties are just starting to be promoted by hotels, department stores, and travel destinations. (Las Vegas is a natural for such things.) Our society is in the infant stages of developing cultural rituals for divorce. Perhaps there's a role for business to play in the development of these rituals. Gatherings and "celebrations" are appealing because women want support and good wishes as they embark on their next phase of life. There are opportunities for all kinds of businesses, from gyms to salons, spas, and even those selling food products and apparel, to promote "reinvention" programs to help fuel the confidence and positive energy that newly divorced women are seeking.

- **With each geographic move comes the inevitable need for new furniture, new gadgets, and newly stocked pantries.**

Retailers should not only have wedding registries but also consider some form of divorce registries, so that women can help friends and relatives select gifts they really need. Not only do people have to replace what they've lost in the divorce, they usually want to add other new things as well, so that the realignment feels like a positive beginning.

From a broader standpoint, divorced parents of school-age children require duplicates of every kind of kid gear (making two-for-one promotions highly appealing), not to mention furnishings for the kids' second bedroom in the other parent's new household and all the toys, food, books, paint, art, mops, brooms, hammers, and cleaning gear needed to stock and decorate the new place.

- **Divorced women have special needs in certain categories.**

Among the industries most significantly affected are:

Financial services. Banks and insurance companies have an opportunity to promote "divorce specialists" to help clients navigate the complex waters of planning for a future that was never anticipated.

Employment. There's also a tremendous opportunity to employ the legions of women who've retained primary custody of their children but can't afford full-time child care. Call-center staffing companies and direct-selling firms such as Jafra, Arbonne, and Avon are great examples of companies that have capitalized on this labor force by enabling women to work from home. The airline Jet Blue, for example, has about 700 at-home reservation agents in Salt Lake City.

An easier way for kids to travel alone. Heaven knows

the world needs more airline and airport services for children traveling alone to visit noncustodial parents. Attention to details such as family bathrooms and baby-changing stations inside men's bathrooms is a huge help for when dads have custody.

The Presence of More Older Women Redefines Target Markets

Rosemarie Brennan is a popular figure in the real estate circles of Austin, Texas. She can be seen tooling around town in her shiny Lexus SUV, hammering For Sale signs in the front yards of houses all over the northwestern part of the city. When she's not working, she's out having lunch with her girlfriends, working out with her personal trainer, shopping at her favorite store, Stein Mart, and throwing dinner parties. She recently got back from a holiday adventure in Australia, where she spent three weeks touring the country. She's contemplating joining a local singles group but isn't sure if she can find the time. Besides, she's not interested in getting married—though finding a travel or dinner companion might be nice. She attends adult-education classes at the University of Texas every Friday.

Rosemarie is a sixty-nine-year-old widow. In addition to being my mother, she is representative of the new breed of older woman: active, engaged in life, credit-card-wielding, and in charge of the household purse strings.

In America, marketers tend to put older people in a "ghetto"—in this case, an imaginary place where all people over the age of forty-nine (the cutoff age for many advertising briefs) are frail, senile, set in their ways, waving their canes around at young people, and generally not worth targeting. This is an old model of thinking that urgently needs to be revised around the new reality of global aging.

In the United States, there are more baby boomer women (born between 1946 and 1964) than Generation X women (born between 1965 and 1980). This makes it astonishing that so many companies limit their target market to people ages eighteen to fifty-four. Our obsession with youth is blinding us. Aging is a consumer opportunity around the world, not just in Western countries. South Korea, Thailand, Taiwan, and Singapore will have an average population age of forty in 2050. Japan has the oldest population in the world. The impact that older people will have on society, lifestyles, retirement, housing, medicine, and consumer spending has only just begun.[28] Since women live an average of five to ten years longer than men, you can guess who makes up the majority of older people.

Financially speaking, people over age fifty have the greatest assets and highest net worth of any group in the United States. It makes sense, since these people have spent a lifetime earning, investing, and accumulating money. According to the American Association of Retired People (AARP), individuals over fifty own 79 percent of all financial assets and control 80 percent of all the money in savings accounts, 62 percent of all large Wall Street investment accounts, and 66 percent of all dollars in the stock market.

Baby boomer women, who live longer than their husbands, stand to inherit money from both their parents and their spouses over the next twenty years. Looking at the aging population and the amount of money it controls—

even when recent stock market losses are factored in—a huge crop of new business opportunities reveals itself, especially when one considers that most boomers intend to keep working well into retirement age.[29] When it comes to consumer spending, youth really is overrated.

By far the most consistently overlooked demographic anywhere, this group of women has more time, and in many cases a greater willingness to spend money on consumer products, than any other group in history. As a cohort that was catered to throughout their younger lives, some feel particularly disenchanted that marketers are so clearly ignoring them now. In business terms, of course, this is an opportunity.

In 2006, Unilever's Dove brand turned stereotypes upside down through its advertising depictions of real women across the age and weight spectrum. This well-publicized breakthrough campaign was created after the company conducted a global study on aging and perceptions of beauty. The study found that 91 percent of women ages fifty to sixty-four felt that media and advertising need to do a better job of presenting realistic images of women over fifty. Nearly 60 percent of the women felt that if magazines were deemed reflective of a population, a reader could likely believe that women over fifty do not exist.[30] When it comes to pop culture, many feel invisible.

These findings were of little surprise to women; the news value came from the fact that no major brand had ever discussed the issue so publicly before. As consumers, we're so conditioned to looking at ads featuring nearly nude teenage models airbrushed to perfection that it's easy to forget that almost nobody actually looks like that. Where, on the other hand, are all the people who are aging gracefully, such as actress Diane Keaton (born in 1946)? A look at any magazine or television show is proof that such individuals are virtually nonexistent in the media, except in "silver fox" commercials for products such as adult diapers, vitamins, and Medicare supplements. Remember the old television ad "I've fallen and I can't get up"? It was a pure distillation of the elderly stereotype, and it stuck like a piece of Velcro in people's minds as the image of what it means to be old.

A major AARP study of women ages forty-five to ninety shows that they consider themselves to be happier now than they've ever been, thus debunking the myth that the second half of life is not as good as the first, particularly for women.[31] In many ways, women feel a sense of freedom as they get older—freedom from society's expectations that they behave in a certain way, and freedom from the pressure to remain sexually attractive to young men. Older women don't have to seek approval from others anymore. They're free to be themselves, and that is one of the most liberating feelings anyone can have, no matter which gender.

From these data you can draw some insights for business:

- **There's a big difference between being youthful and being young.**

Older women feel good about themselves and aren't trying to look like they're twenty; in fact, most are relieved that they're not.

No matter what the mirror tells them, many older people feel younger on the inside and want products that help them maintain that feeling. This attitude represents untapped opportunities for businesses, and not just the usual suspects in the cosmetics industry. How about "hip" underwear and other products that address the unsexy effects of aging, such as incontinence? At the time of this writing, personal-products giant Kimberly-Clark has announced that it's overhauling its Depend line of disposable underwear for men and women, in anticipation of an influx of aging Americans. For the first time in its twenty-five-year history, the Depend brand is featuring separate versions of absorbent underwear, with different leg openings and other changes, to fit men's and women's bodies.[32]

It's just the tip of the iceberg. Where are the cool-looking technology products with bigger buttons, higher sound volumes, and larger fonts on LCD panels? Designer "orthopedic" shoes? (How long can Taryn Rose and Aerosoles be the only brands out there?) Where are the cool clothes for the aging woman? If you're over the age of fifty, trying to find a pair of jeans isn't easy. Take your mom out shopping one weekend to see what I mean. It's brutal, and it doesn't get any easier at ages sixty, seventy, or eighty.

Consider what a broadened definition of luxury could mean to this group of people, who still feel young and vital. Ironically, luxury is largely absent from the world of products for the over-fifty crowd, and yet this is the segment with money to spend.

From an advertising standpoint, the balance between youthful and realistic portrayals of people in this age group can be a tough call, because women of every age still like to see images that make them feel youthful and attractive. But remember, youthful isn't the same thing as young. Women will respond positively to photographs of older women who look wonderful. Last year, when fifty-one-year-old Ellen DeGeneres was named the new face of CoverGirl, it was the next logical step in the movement of celebrating real women whom people admire for more than just their youth and cheekbones.

- **Baby boomer women are open to new brands and products and aren't necessarily stuck on the brands they loved decades ago.**

Are you still buying the same brands you bought twenty years ago? Probably not. As people mature, so do their tastes. And as they get older and (very likely) earn more money, there is the added benefit of the Internet providing exposure to new brands and products every day.

Unfortunately, there's an ingrained belief in marketing that older people can't change their brand preferences; this may be a hangover impression from the spending habits of the baby boomers' parents, who lived through the Great Depression. It certainly doesn't apply to baby boomers themselves, especially women.

Empty-nester women have money to spend on themselves, and for many of them, it's the first time in their lives they don't have to put themselves last, behind the kids. My mother surprised us all when she bought a new Lexus SUV after her five kids had grown up and left the house. She had driven station wagons and boring sedans her whole life. We never knew she would have preferred a hot car all along. (Aren't all children guilty of viewing their parents as existing solely for them?)

By this stage of life, it's important to understand that older women already have lots of "stuff," and what they really value is the ability to collect new experiences and memories. They feel a sense of joy and excitement at this stage of life, because so many opportunities are open to them, especially if they've maintained their health. Generally speaking, they possess a hunger to learn, travel, and become more educated, and gravitate toward companies and brands that help them do just that.

• **Health and wellness are important concerns for older women. Most fear becoming a burden to those they love.**

From yoga classes to water aerobics and running in groups, older women are finding ways to stay active. Since 1990, there has been a 411 percent increase in the population of health club members over the age of fifty-five.[33]

Curves is a successful fitness company that's bucked the trend of targeting eighteen- to thirty-four-year-old consumers. The company attracts the typically gym-shy, forty-plus female consumer with its women-only clubs that have a low-key, unintimidating environment. All the clubs feature thirty-minute workouts, and this formula has worked. Curves is the fastest-growing fitness franchise in the world. It now sells Curves-branded apparel, footwear, and workout gear through direct-sales giant Avon, as well as Curves-branded cereal and snacks through General Mills. It's effectively extended its brand so that members can live the Curves lifestyle outside of its fitness facilities. And most important, it's brought a lot of older women into the gym who might not otherwise have joined.

• **Older people don't see themselves reflected in American culture.**

Feeling connected is a huge part of feeling healthy and vital. But it can be hard to feel connected when you look around at the big wide world and don't see yourself reflected back in the media. The American pop culture environment is pretty sparse when it comes to movies, television shows, magazine spreads, and radio networks that target the over-fifty crowd. When you travel to other countries, one of the first things you notice is that people on TV—whether they're news presenters or actors in soap operas such as Britain's long-running *Coronation Street*—represent a wider range of ages (especially older ones and especially women) than are typically seen in the United States. We're missing the boat, and all the dollars that come along with that boat.

- **Older people often help more with their grandkids than they ever could have imagined they would.**

Grandparent contributions of time and money have become an economic force. In many families, grandparents greatly assist with child care, education costs, and the funding of the kids' "extras." Studies show that as many as 22 percent of grandparents are helping to pay college tuition for their grandkids.[34] Addressing grandparents as an audience when selling products and services for kids is a smart idea—because they might be the only adults in the family who can afford them.

GENERATION XXXL

There's no real need to look at obesity statistics when a stroll through any American mall will do. We're getting bigger as a nation and a planet. Our adults are big, our kids are big, and even our pets are big. (There is a burgeoning market in controlling pet obesity, but I digress.)

Women have higher obesity rates than men, according to the Centers for Disease Control. More than one-third of women ages twenty to seventy-four are obese.[35] The rates are even higher for Mexican American women (52 percent) and African American women (53 percent). We all know that female obesity carries a greater social stigma than its male counterpart. Women are expected to be thin and beautiful, while men are forgiven for being heavy and bald. It's a classic double standard. Obesity, however, knows no age: about 27 percent of kids in the United States are currently considered obese, and often they are the children of obese parents.[36]

In America, the average weight for a woman is 164 pounds.[37] This is a nearly twenty-five-pound increase since 1960. (Women also grew an inch taller during this time, with the average height shifting from 5'3" to 5'4".) The health impact of obesity is well documented, but its implications for industries that sell to women have been less reported. Few have examined the subject from a consumer-products point of view, with the notable exceptions of the food and diet industries. Obesity is a global problem, and ironically, developing countries have to battle food on two fronts, by trying to eliminate both obesity and malnutrition at the same time. Obesity rates have tripled in Great Britain since 1982, more than doubled in Australia, and risen 97 percent in China in the past decade.[38]

What's driving this unfortunate trend? The usual suspects—a sedentary lifestyle combined with over-sized portions of unhealthy, processed food. Americans work more hours than any other population in the industrialized world. Logging nearly 2,000 hours of work each year, most Americans find it difficult to find the time to exercise and eat right. When combined with women's typically busy schedules, which often include transporting kids, cooking, cleaning, shopping, and scheduling the cable installer, the outlook is pretty bleak that the tide will reverse itself anytime soon. When you look back at a day in the life of Jamie, whose schedule was documented earlier in this chapter, it's hard to imagine where she might be able to squeeze in some quality exercise and cooking time. She says she does, but not as often as she'd like.

Our extreme eating habits and huge portions are driving us to spend ever more money to get the weight off. Between $33 billion and $55 billion is already spent annually on weight-loss products and services.[39] Life Time Fitness is a fast-growing business in the United States that caters to the fitness and nutritional needs of families. In enormous "gyms" averaging 110,000 square feet—which can only be described as a cross between a country club and a mall—whole families participate in healthy activities ranging from eating low-carb meals in its restaurants to attending Pilates classes and swimming lessons. While at the club, members can check their e-mail via Wi-Fi, get a quick haircut at the center's Aveda salon, or drink a hot beverage at Caribou Coffee—all while a professional staff watches the kids in a supervised child care center. The company has nearly one hundred locations in the United States.

Life Time Fitness has created a new format that caters to the modern (and more often than not plump) American family. Such fitness multiplexes offer something for everyone, making it easy for mothers to take their families along with them while they work out. The gyms are beautiful and stigma-free, and designed for the reality of modern family lives.

Insights for business:

- **Plus-size women are becoming the norm in the United States.**

The average American woman is a size fourteen, and the numbers aren't expected to change anytime soon—though this reality is not reflected broadly in apparel offerings or media portrayals. Women of all sizes want beautiful clothes, elegant bridal gowns, lovely prom dresses, fashionable shoes, and cool workout gear. They don't want to wear frumpy clothes any more than thin women do. If a woman wears a large dress size, it means that her hands and feet are larger, too, creating implications for shoes, jewelry, and handbag design, as well as furniture, housewares, and even cars.

- **Helping women solve their time conundrum is the key to helping them eat well and work out.**

Finding ways to help women manage their family and work responsibilities in order to exercise or eat well is a compelling offering that companies such as Life Time Fitness and Curves are leveraging for profit.

- **Larger women will often invest in makeup, nail, and hair care products, because these are for parts of the body unaffected by their weight.**

This is one theory behind the explosion of nail salons across the country. If someone has a hard time controlling her weight, she'll take care of the parts of her body she *can* control—her hair, nails, and skin. It's another possible explanation for the irrationally large amounts of handbags and shoes that flood the market every season. A purse or shoe will almost always fit, and one doesn't need a potentially humiliating trip to the dressing room to try them on.

Women Around the World:
The Importance of Cultural Context

WHEN you think of the immense variety in the lives of women around the world, it's helpful to view different countries as being on a continuum of progress. Industrialized nations are the most progressive when it comes to women's participation in the public sphere, and this is reflected in the robustness of their economies. The emerging economies of India, China, Russia, and Brazil still lag behind the industrialized nations but are making headway. Unsurprisingly, most developing countries still have a long way to go when it comes to enabling women to become full contributors to their economies. History tells us that women's participation in the commercial economy follows a pattern:

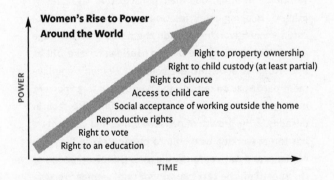

When it comes to global growth and expansion, many Western companies have India and China firmly in their crosshairs. It's worth taking a moment to look at the lives of women in those nations from a top-line perspective. They are the power purchasers of the emerging economies.

THE WOMEN OF INDIA

Having made two trips to India to better understand the country's women and its culture, I left with more questions than answers. If there is one country that defies generalizations, it's India. With multitudes of languages, religions, traditions, cuisines, and forms of entertainment, it's endlessly colorful and nearly impossible to pin down. There are, however, some broad themes impacting the women of India that are important to understand for any company entering the market. The crux of the matter is this: Indian women, especially those of the middle and upper classes, are caught squarely between modernity and tradition.

It's true that women are slowly entering the paid workforce in India, but their participation lags that of other developing countries. Some still frown upon educated women working outside the home after marriage and childbirth, but more women continue to take jobs as opportunities pour into the country. Women's employment participation outside the home grew to 31 percent in 2005 from 26 percent in 2000, the first rise seen in decades.[40] The growth of private airlines and call centers has thrust working women into public view as flight attendants and call-center employees. On the other end of the spectrum, the vast majority of rural women are self-employed, engaged in activities such as growing food, making handicrafts, and doing all manner of work to bring money into their families. Countless millions of women work at the subsistence level in rural India.

In this hierarchical society, wife and mother are still the most highly valued roles a woman can play, no matter what her caste (hereditary social class). Women wield a tremendous amount of "informal" authority in the private sphere. They consider themselves to be the primary decision makers for their families in almost every consumer category. With nearly five hundred million women in the country, to say that Indian women are an economic force is kind of like saying Bollywood makes a lot of movies—it's an understatement.

Culturally speaking, women are subject to an enormous amount of social control. There are implicit and explicit behavioral codes, social codes, and religious codes that they're expected to follow. Women in their late thirties and forties in particular struggle with this. "Our mothers are living the traditional roles," says Shefalee Vasudev, editor of *Marie Claire* magazine in India. "Some daughters rebel totally, some rebel partially, and some don't rebel at all. There are curbs on personal freedom and codes for women. It won't be resolved in one generation. The generations after us—the ones to come—will have it easier."

The primary religion in India is Hinduism, but the country also has one of the most enormous Muslim populations in the world. Socially, India is conservative, especially when it comes to love and romance. Dating openly is rare, and public displays of affection are frowned upon, even between married couples. Indian movies have only started showing a chaste kiss between two characters within the past decade. Homosexuality is not discussed, and its existence is rarely acknowledged. Women are expected to be pure and chaste.

MARRIAGE: THE DEFINITION OF SUCCESS FOR YOUNG WOMEN

A young woman before marriage is considered "held in trust" by her parents. Most women (and men) live with their parents until they get married. When women marry, it's not uncommon for them to move in with their husband's parents and become their caregivers. The average age of marriage is still just under twenty. In Indian society, marriage is the most important part of a person's life, and from the time a baby is born, his or her parents worry about making a good match for the child. Even among the wealthiest classes, who may send their daughters to college abroad, a good marriage is often considered more important than a good career. However, new research shows that most housewives now want to be wage-earning women. This new attitude is combined with a slowdown in India's birthrate (which makes it easier for women to work outside the home) as well as increasing social legitimacy for women's education. Businesses, in the form of "office jobs," provide a socially acceptable space for women to participate in the public sphere alongside men. However, working in retail or in restaurants and coffee shops is considered lower-class work that is inappropriate for well-raised young women.

THE IMPORTANCE OF FAMILY

Family is the most important aspect of Indian life, and this is reflected throughout Indian culture, including the thousand or so Indian films that are produced every year. The concept of a nuclear family is new to India and is being driven by the increasing wealth of the middle classes. Most people live in extended-family arrangements, but young people with "new" money and career women are establishing beachheads for the concept of living as a nuclear family.

Men are kings of the Indian family, and a baby boy is what every young woman wants and is often pressured by her family to produce. Society tells women they should have sons, and the message is not so subtly conveyed in advertisements, on television, and in movie plots. In fact, the problem of aborting female fetuses is so widespread— especially among the most affluent classes—that the government of India passed a law that's made it illegal for doctors to disclose the sex of a fetus to the parents during an ultrasound.[41]

Men are accustomed to being waited on by their female family members, which is why it can be difficult for more traditional men to accept their wives going off to the workplace. Their parents also expect to be taken care of by their new daughters-in-law, so women have pressure coming from all sides. From the male perspective, men have little to gain when their wives go off to work. As magazine editor Vasudev puts it, "It's hard for men to give up the crown."

URBAN VERSUS RURAL

A wealthy person in Mumbai has more in common with someone from New York than with someone from rural India. Something on the order of 30 percent of India's citizens live on less than a dollar a day, while others live like royalty. The eight megacities of India where most Western companies have focused their efforts are Mumbai, Delhi, Kolkata, Hyderabad, Bangalore, Chennai, Ahmedabad, and Pune. However, there is new interest in smaller cities, which are full of people who may have more time on their hands than the busy folks in the big cities and who have plenty of aspirations. On conservative estimates, 379 million people will be added to India's urban spaces over the next forty years—more than the entire population of the United States today.[42]

THE MODERN INDIAN WOMAN

From a commerce perspective, Indian women have been understudied, but things are changing, and old stereotypes are starting to give way to reality. "Indian women are seeking 'space retrieval,' which is their own individual space in the world, but not at the expense of someone else," explains Santosh Desai, CEO of Future Brands and one of the country's best-known advertising professionals. "Before, there was nothing left over for a woman; she was exhausted by all her duties," he says. "Now there is something left over for herself. This is a change. There is a sense of confidence and self restraint that comes from being able to navigate the world."

RETAIL IN INDIA

Credit card penetration is low in India, and this impacts consumers' ability to make large purchases on credit. Online shopping is not popular yet. For Indians, at least for now, shopping is a visceral experience, with people jostling elbow to elbow for the best bargains. Shopping in India is all about energy, crowds, and hubbub. Many Indians view Western retail as boring and passive. As Future Brands' Desai puts it, "In India, we just don't respond to the concept of retail as art installation."

The bottom line is that with higher rates of female employment, dropping fertility rates, and a fast-rising middle class, the drivers are in place for women to play an even greater economic role in India. The challenge for international businesses will be to appeal to India's strong sense of culture and pride. Mumbai-based, American-born Roopa Purushothaman, currently one of the rising young stars in the world of economics, explained a popular saying to me. "No one ever comes here and changes India," she said. "You come here and get changed."

THE WOMEN OF CHINA

Modern China has placed an emphasis on gender equality that is unique among countries. Chinese women have been in the workforce ever since 1949, when Mao Zedong took power and declared, "Women hold up half the sky." Mao established equality between the sexes (at least theoretically) under Communism. Nearly all women who wanted work found employment in state-run factories, which offered free schools and day care for workers' children. Women found themselves with jobs in engineering, science, the military, and agricultural work.

In the 1950s and 1960s, when the stereotype of June Cleaver–style housewives was grabbing hold in the West, China could not have been more different. Its women marched off to work in gray Mao jackets and hats while singing songs in praise of the Party. Then the Cultural Revolution began in 1965, ushering in a tumultuous era of violence and fear. In 1979, the one-child policy was enacted to curb the population explosion. Then, ever so slowly, China started opening up its big red gates to the world.

YOUNG WOMEN DRIVE CONSUMER GROWTH

Fast-forward to today. Urban Chinese women are driving the consumer goods explosion in China. Walking through the streets of Shanghai, I felt an overwhelming need to increase my fashion sensibility just to keep up with all the trendy women rushing through the streets, talking animatedly on their cell phones. In particular, women ages thirty-one to forty are the most powerful force to be reckoned with. They outspend all others on beauty, entertainment, travel, cosmetics, clothing, and books.[43]

These women crave luxury products and brands, and dress themselves in status symbols to show the world they're successful.

Their younger counterparts, the first generation of children raised after China's one-child policy was enacted in 1979, are now spending money alongside them as they fill the ranks of the urban Chinese workforce. Chinese women are embracing the kind of self-expression that once was unimaginable in this country—from fashion, art, music, and blogging to writing openly about sex and money. There is a generational divide between women over forty, who lived through the deprivations of the Cultural Revolution, and the younger women who have come after them. The former are more apt to save money in case the bad times return; the latter want to spend it because they have only experienced good times.

A GENERATION OF "LITTLE EMPERORS"

Women born after 1979, who are now age thirty and younger, grew up in a different world than their older counterparts. Raised as only children, they've had the benefit of six adults—one set of parents and two sets of grandparents—involved in every aspect of their lives. Thus they are accustomed to being on the receiving end of adults' attention and money. This generation of kids has been nicknamed the "little emperors" and is considered to be spoiled—especially the boys. Because they live with their parents until they get married, these young people often have proportionally more disposable income than their counterparts in other parts of the world, who have to pay for rent and food. The resulting explosion in young women's spending has been characterized in the international media as the "pink yuan."

With China's vast aging population, however, it's not

just the younger women who have the money. Empty-nester women are predicted to have U.S. $150 billion of purchasing power in 2015, while their younger counterparts will likely have U.S. $260 billion in spending power in the same time frame.[44] The health and beauty industry is feeling the impact of all this spending because it's the first point of entry for women who want to buy luxury brands. Very few companies are paying attention to the forty-plus market in China, and these women represent an enormous opportunity, as they do in Western countries.

WOMEN SPEND THE FAMILY MONEY

Like India, family is the axis upon which China revolves. People live in extended families with their parents and grandparents and feel a strong sense of responsibility for the well-being of their family's older members. Like everywhere else in the world, women are the shoppers in Chinese families. An estimated 78 percent of married women make the decisions for grocery, apparel, and other essential purchases for their families, and 77 percent say their opinions are important when it comes to buying big-ticket items with their husbands.[45]

With the one-child policy still in place, families remain small, and women find it relatively easy to stay in the workforce after childbirth. (There is usually a grandparent around who can help with child care.) A study from the China Women's Federation and the National Statistics Bureau shows that even if they had a husband with a high salary, 88 percent of women would choose to work.[46]

NO THANKS; MAYBE LATER?

More and more urban Chinese women are postponing marriage and children. The average age of first marriage is twenty-six for women in the capital, Beijing—about two years older than a decade ago.[47] The country is facing a social time bomb in the years to come, since the preference of Chinese for male children means that young men now dramatically outnumber young women. There are currently 121 boys for every 100 girls.[48] Along with delayed marriage comes the phenomenon of divorce, which is rising in Chinese cities. Many urban divorces are blamed on the rise of mistresses, who are called *ernai*. Mistresses have become a status symbol for successful Chinese businessmen. In fact, there are many who believe the "mistress economy"—the habit of buying gifts for one's mistress—is the single biggest factor driving the adoption of luxury goods in China's big cities.

In both China and India, middle-class women have latent needs—they don't necessarily know what they want yet, because they haven't been exposed to many of the products and services we take for granted in the West. Multinational companies are now skimming the top of the population for wealthy consumers, but the greatest opportunities for both countries are with the "smaller" cities (a relative term) and the rising middle class. The size of China's burgeoning middle class is hotly debated, but by some estimates it's predicted to reach a hundred million by 2016, up from thirty-five million today.[49]

Whether It's Beijing or Baltimore, New Delhi or North Carolina, Women's Consumer Domination Is Here for the Long Term

THE global trends driving women's educational attainment, workforce participation, and subsequent purchasing patterns mean that women are expected to dominate the consumer economy for the next twenty-five years or longer. Studying the trends among women of all age groups will lead to a better understanding of how to deliver the goods and services that women want. As you begin the process of catering to the alpha consumer, keep in mind the new paradigm of the female consumer world order:

- Women dominate spending in virtually every consumer-products category.
- The person who makes a sales transaction isn't necessarily the decision maker. Even if the woman of the house does not earn a paycheck, she likely determines the household's expenditures.
- Women are raised in a different gender culture than men are, and their priorities and worldviews are different. The female culture should be studied with the same focus and intensity that entering a foreign market requires.
- Success for most global consumer-products companies lies in female hands.

Now that you've got an idea of where women are going, it's time to look at companies that are already designing products to take them there.

4

PINK IS NOT
A STRATEGY

Creating Products with a
Female Focus

In all that's been written about the brilliance of Apple, one aspect of the company's success has rarely been mentioned: that it just may be the world's most discreetly feminine brand.

Take the iPod: it completely feminized the dude-driven world of stereo equipment. Small, beautiful, curvy, easy to use (no manual necessary), intuitive, and colorful, it's everything that stereo equipment never was. The Shuffle version of the iPod is like the Volkswagen Beetle of the product line, and a magnet for women. The stereotype of the nerdy guy audiophile, with his mysterious knowledge of woofers, tweeters, and amps, has been replaced by women in workout gear running to their favorite songs on shiny teal Shuffles. Traditional stereo shops seem as out of date as the Victrola, and stand in contrast to Apple stores, which are light, bright, and bursting with women. It's hard to imagine that Nick Hornby could have written *High Fidelity* in the age of the iPod.

Slowly, women's consumer dominance is transforming one industry after another. Consumer electronics is probably the most visible because of the abundance of pink phones and laptops, but even traditional industries such as household goods are being reshaped to their changing needs. (Witness the Swiffer, which we'll cover in the pages ahead.) Women represent a massive opportunity for classically "male" industries to reach a new target audience and reinvigorate flat businesses. WD-40's No Mess Pen, for example, has been created to enable people to carry around the lubricant—a mainstay of toolboxes—in purses and pockets. Much has been written about women's shopping habits online and off, but their impact on the economy extends to product development itself. There is still an enormous opportunity to design products to better appeal to women.

Pink Is Not a Strategy

THERE are two common mistakes people make when creating products intended for women. The first is to simply create pink versions of existing products, and the second is to try to market existing products to women without sufficiently adapting them to their needs.

Women are underrepresented in the fields of industrial design and engineering, so the feminine point of view is often absent in product development. Products that claim "macho" bragging rights to being bigger, faster, or stronger typically don't impress women. When it comes to "unisex" product categories, women want to know what something will do for them, how it will make their life better in some way, and how it will impact the people important to them; if it looks great, that's all the better. There's an old Shaker expression that captures the idea perfectly: "Don't make something unless it is both necessary and useful, but if it is both necessary and useful, don't hesitate to make it beautiful."

Does it need to be pink? No. Do women want a pink option sometimes? Sure. I love pink, and so do lots of women, but there are also millions who find it disappointing that the color of fairy princesses and Pepto-Bismol has somehow been designated the universal color for females. (Just try to buy a little girl a present that isn't pink.) Women have a tempestuous relationship with the color. (See sidebar on page 157.) And while it's true that many pink versions of unisex products are successful, such as pink iPods and cell phones, they do well because women actually like their design and performance, not just the rosy hue.

When a product is offered in only one color, and that color is pink, it sends the message, *We haven't put any thought into this at all.* A notable exception is when a product is raising money for breast cancer research, which, of course, is a wonderful cause. In fact, much of pink's recent pervasiveness stems from such fund-raising, or from attempts to ride its coattails. But unless your company is trying to raise money for research into the disease, it's best to consider pink as simply one color offering among many. Pink is style, not substance, and it doesn't pass for a design strategy. Someday the current glut of pink products will be looked back on as the first stage of manufacturers' response to the rising power of women.

> ## The Lesson of Swiffer:
> ## In the right hands, observing the obvious
> ## is golden

Myth: Women will tell you everything you want.
Reality: It's better to watch what they do instead.

What do women want from your product?

The short answer is everything you've promised them. But getting to that point—actually determining what they need and want—is where the magic of good research comes in. And one of the most effective methods for studying women is observation, or what's often called ethnographic research, the art of watching people in their natural habitat.

Procter & Gamble is a standout in this method of research. In 2005, the company's CEO, A. G. Lafley, was the subject of a page-one feature story in the *Wall Street Journal* in which he declared that women were the heart of the company's new turnaround strategy. A lot of people read the article and thought: *For heaven's sake, if P&G doesn't know how to market to women, who does?* After all, it's the world's largest consumer-products company and the world's largest advertiser, and its customers are overwhelmingly women. But Lafley explained that even though women have been the company's target consumers for more than 170 years, he felt the corporate culture had been too internally focused and hadn't done enough to understand their needs.

P&G's traditional formula was to create products in an R&D lab and then trot them out to the marketplace, promoting their technical and performance benefits. Lafley instituted a reverse process—finding out what women want through real-life observation in their homes, and then head-ing back to the R&D labs to create the products. He also set a goal that half of all new products would come from outside the company. From 2002 to 2007, P&G invested $1 billion in consumer research, talking to more than four million customers each year.[1] During the same period, its stock price soared, rising nearly two-thirds in value and setting new highs.

P&G employees will actually live with consumers in their homes and shop with them as they run their errands through an internal immersion program called Living It. Another program, called Working It, gives employees the opportunity to work behind the counter at small shops.[2] When it comes to consumer research, P&G goes deep.

Swiffer, Procter & Gamble's mega cleaning brand and one of the great category disrupters, is a stunning example of the company's ability to determine women's unarticulated needs.

If you're not familiar with Swiffer, it's a line of cleaning products for mopping, sweeping, and dusting that has become a business and pop-culture phenomenon, appearing on everything from *Saturday Night Live* to the cover of *Rolling Stone* magazine. Swiffer is the Mick Jagger of mops. P&G's use of observational research played a significant role in the development of the product line, which is now in more than fifty million households.[3] Supported by a fun, pop-music-filled marketing campaign, Swiffer is well on its way to becoming one of P&G's billion-dollar brands.

I interviewed one of the executives in charge of Swiffer, and the first thing you notice when talking to someone at Procter & Gamble is the unwavering use of the pronoun "she." P&G is focused like a laser beam on women.

The idea for Swiffer came from detailed observations of

women mopping kitchen floors. Researchers from the company's Mr. Clean team noticed that women spent serious amounts of time prepping their floors for mopping, as well as wringing out their dirty mops over and over again. They also learned just how much women hated touching a filthy, wet mop. If you've ever mopped, you know that when it's time to squeeze the dirty water out of the mop head, or pour it out of the bucket, it's almost impossible to avoid spilling it on yourself. Through its research, P&G also identified a trend it found intriguing: a rise in what the company calls the "ick" factor—the negative feelings around messy household chores.

"Cleaning was seen as drudgery, a thankless task, particularly for surface-cleaning areas," says Kent Lynde, the executive who runs P&G's surface-care business globally, of which Swiffer is the crown jewel. Mopping, in particular, was dreaded, and the negative feelings around it were getting worse. "We had to find out what that was all about," explains Lynde.

There was a simple answer. P&G found that women's increasing level of workforce participation (global trend #1) was driving a parallel increase in the "ick" factor, particularly around the mop-and-bucket process. "Women were thinking, 'My lifestyle is now changing, and I don't have time to deal with this bucket and water and all this mess and all these germs," says Lynde.

There's a certain brilliance in realizing that if P&G could find a solution to a universal problem—*mopping sucks*—everyone would love it.

Finding Gold in the Mundane

By paying close attention to something so unpleasant that most of us would think it hardly worth a second thought, P&G went on to create one of its top-selling brands, which in the world's largest consumer-products company is really saying something. The classic Swiffer (there are many variations now) is made with electrostatic sheets that can be tossed into the garbage after use. It's essentially "bucketless mopping"—no water, no squeezing, no sloshing. The process is odorless, clean, and easy. The word *Swiffer* is now a verb. And the brand is built on the lucrative razor-and-blades model of buying one handle and replenishing it with refills and pads. People hadn't realized mopping could be done any other way—until P&G.

Swiffer's success shows us how important it is to watch people interact with products in the context of their real lives—not just in corporate labs or R&D facilities. Many executives also rely too heavily on traditional feedback methods such as focus groups, in which participants may feel pressure to say what they think the moderator wants to hear, or conform to group opinion.

Lynde and his team consider observational research to be particularly valuable when it comes to new-to-the-world products. "Simulations are not that helpful to us. We have to know what's really going on, and she can't always say it. A survey can't give you that," he says. Originally, the Mr. Clean team had begun studying the "wet cleaning" process because that was the domain of its brand. By watching women, they started to learn about the "dry cleaning" process—the prep work that's done before mopping the floor—and that's what sparked the idea that led to Swiffer.

THE CONSUMER LED US THERE

"Originally, our insight into the category was all around wet cleaning," Lynde explains. "P&G wasn't in vacuum cleaners. We weren't in brooms. But watching women prep for mopping was how we got the concept for our very first Swiffer product. We never had the intention of doing anything like that when we went into the research process. If we had a technology-led or product-led approach to R&D (as opposed to consumer-led), we never would have gotten there."

I asked Lynde to name the one thing P&G never does in consumer research. His answer: "We never ask, *'What kind of product would you like to have?'* We constantly learn that consumers don't know a better life. They only know the current world." It reminds me of that famous Henry Ford quote: "If I'd asked my customers what they wanted, they would have said a faster horse."

Almost all the traditional research methods are used at P&G, but many of its new-to-the-world ideas are hatched during in-home visits. "We're always developing new products that have never existed before," says Lynde. "So we use a lot of different research methods to get there. How we innovate is just as important as what we innovate." Lynde notes that P&G can't rely on in-home studies 100 percent of the time because of the Heisenberg Uncertainty Principle— or the Observer Effect—which means one's observation of someone during an experiment can affect the experiment itself. It's kind of like the difference between the first series of MTV's *Real World,* which was genuinely fascinating, to the later ones, in which everyone is hamming for the camera.

Here's a great example of the new-product pipeline that observational research can yield: Lynde and his team were in a consumer's home testing a Swiffer product one day when the woman told them that Swiffer was the first product she'd ever used that was light enough for her to lift up and reach the cobwebs in the corner of her ceiling. At that point, she lifted the product to the ceiling to show the researchers how she did it. That insight was the spark that led to the creation of the Swiffer Duster XL, which is elongated to help people reach those tricky ceiling corners.

THE ICING ON THE CAKE: THOUGHTFUL FEATURES THAT MAKE THE DIFFERENCE

Truly great products don't just solve a problem; they offer an element of delight. That's what separates the billion-dollar brands from the chaff. "This element of delight is something we very much focus on, because it's beyond the rational when it comes to purchasing decisions," says Lynde.

"Delight" is just a euphemism for thoughtful details. As with every other aspect of their lives, women notice the thoughtful details in product design. "From the moment she opens the Swiffer box, she has to say, 'Ah, I get it. It's even better than they said,'" notes Lynde. "That's our goal. And that only comes through adding the elements of delight beyond the functional perfection that we try to achieve in our products."

Some of Swiffer's details that women notice and appreciate include:

- Textures and features on the mops that prevent them from falling over when they're leaning against a wall
- Velcro on Wet Jet pads that allows users to throw the pad on the ground and stamp it onto the mop, without having to turn the mop upside down

- A 360-degree turning radius on the heads of the mops, for getting around furniture legs and tough corners more easily

Today, P&G employees spend hours with ordinary women, watching them wash their clothes, clean their houses, feed their kids, and put on makeup. Researchers look for the small but pesky problems that a new product might solve. To P&G, small and pesky has the potential to mean big and lucrative. Tide to Go stain sticks are another classic example of a great product innovation driven by an unarticulated need. Who says stains occur exclusively in the privacy of your own home? If only. The stick is popular with moms in particular, who find themselves on the receiving end of their kids' spilled juice boxes and other debris. Now they just pop the sticks in their purse, and off they go.

There are several important lessons to be learned from the story of Swiffer that can be used in how you think about creating products for women.

1. **Demographic changes open up new opportunities.**
   As P&G discovered, the fact that more women work outside the home has increased the level of frustration with household chores, creating an opening for a solution like Swiffer. How can you leverage the biggest societal trends (outlined in Chapter 3) to create opportunities for your own business?

2. **If something is a common problem that everyone recognizes, its solution would be universally embraced.**
   Everybody hates mopping. There are lots of things

everybody hates, such as spilling on themselves in public places (a problem that P&G's Tide to Go Sticks solve) and getting wedgies (a problem that Hanes No Ride Up Panties solve). Look for ideas hidden in the obvious, the mundane, the negative, and the bothersome.

3. **Thoughtful details make the difference between a product women like and a product women love.**
   Details are what separate the good from the great. A mop that doesn't tip over when you lean it against the wall? Ingenious.

4. **How you innovate is just as important as what you innovate.**
   Watching your customers in their natural habitat may lead you to innovations faster than simulated environments or written research reports. Since modern women's lives are pulled in so many directions, following them throughout their busy days is one of the most effective ways to determine their unarticulated needs.

5. **Simplicity matters.**
   If the customer needs a manual the size of a Tom Wolfe novel to understand your product, or if industrial-strength scissors are required just to open the package, then you're creating a barrier to women embracing your product. More than a quarter of all households in the United States are run by single women, so there are fewer households in which two adults can be counted on to assemble a product together. Whatever it is, make it easy to open and operate.

Which Approach Is Best: Covert or Overt?

ONE thing everyone knows but rarely talks about is that it's socially acceptable for women to buy products that are clearly made for men, but the reverse is not usually true. For example, in one episode of the TV show *The Office,* Steve Carell's character, the deluded Michael Scott, shows up to work wearing a women's suit he got on sale. Naturally, he is mocked for wearing it, and Scott feels humiliated about "cross-dressing" by accident. Entertainers have long known that the sight gag of men using women's products is good for a laugh, as seen in everything from *Some Like It Hot* to *Monty Python* and *Tootsie.*

It doesn't work the other way around. No one bats an eyelash when a woman throws a man's messenger bag over her shoulder, uses a man's razor on her legs, or wears Chuck Taylor high-tops. But heaven forbid a guy turns up at a gym locker room using his wife's pastel-colored Venus razor—his friends will rib him mercilessly. "We're even afraid to wear pink shirts to work," confides one of my male executive friends who works in a Fortune 500 firm. And he's in marketing, for heaven's sake.

This legitimate fear of turning off men with overtly feminine offerings is one reason executives shy away from creating products and strategies for the women's market. It can be hard to determine whether to execute something *overtly* feminine (such as the Venus razor) or *covertly* feminine (the iPod). Especially when there's no arguing that women love style, color, and fashion in just about everything. So which is the better path for product design, covert or overt?

There is no right answer, but being overtly feminine in a unisex category is riskier, because men are automatically excluded from your market, and a certain percentage of women may feel patronized. No one, man or woman, wants to feel like they're getting a dumbed-down version of a product. However, if you're able to create a product that is genuinely designed for women's needs and it powerfully resonates with them—such as Gillette's Venus brand— then it may make no difference whether or not the men show up; the women could carry you all the way to the bank.

The Lesson of Venus:
Men and women use the same products differently

Myth: Shaving is shaving.
Reality: Addressing real differences can lead to real revenues.

Gillette's Venus is the ultimate example of a winning feminine product born out of an industry traditionally focused on men. This multiblade masterpiece, which now offers up to five blades on a single cartridge, has been a hit since its introduction in 2001 and now commands a whopping 55 percent of the women's razor market.[4] Venus is the number one women's shaving brand in the world, a ranking that has given its competitors a raging case of "Venus Envy," as *BusinessWeek* has dubbed it.

Venus is a proposition of distinct virtues—namely, that it's specially designed for the unique angles and curves of a woman's shaving geography, which is clearly different from men's. Women shave in all sorts of awkward places that men don't, from knees to ankles to armpits and the groin area. There are also differences in how women shave—it's often done standing on one leg in a poorly lit, slippery place, where they must reach awkwardly to get to the parts of the body they can't see, such as armpits and the backs of legs. One actually needs quite a bit of core strength to avoid tumbling right into the tub.

With an elongated, soft-grip handle and pivoting razor head, Venus is ergonomic in all the right places. Today the line offers eight colors, though Venus is often associated with pink because of its advertising campaigns, which position the razor as a beauty product. (Back in 2001, the original launch color was blue, to evoke water.[5]) Regardless of color, Venus has built its success by offering a product that has been designed specifically for women's unique anatomy. The success of Venus teaches three important lessons:

1. **Addressing anatomical differences can lead to new product lines.**

   Venus captured the other half of the population for Gillette by creating a need for a gender-specific product. It communicated its benefits by focusing on the physical differences between men and women. In your own business, it's worth determining whether anatomical differences impact how women use your product, and if there's an opportunity to better leverage these differences. The implications for manufacturers in industries ranging from outdoor clothing and gear (such as backpacks and sleeping bags) to consumer electronics and functional foods, among many others, are enormous and still not fully realized.

2. **There are products in which pink can be used effectively to target women.**

   Not only are pink and the other bright colors in the Venus line cute, they serve a purpose: to keep the men and boys in a woman's household from accidentally using her razor. Wherever you can, however, offer more colors than just pink, so your product doesn't look like a cliché. Venus offers eight colors.

3. **Benefits can be both functional and emotional.**

Venus performs as promised, and it's positioned as a beauty product. Its marketing campaigns tell women Venus will make them more beautiful by unleashing the "goddess" inside them. When a product is created that addresses both functional and emotional benefits, you just may hit the bull's-eye, as Venus did.

THE EVOLUTION OF PINK

For more than twenty years, October has been designated as Breast Cancer Awareness Month, and the sheer number of pink products raising money for the cause means that pink is becoming as symbolic of autumn as the colors of fall leaves. In addition to raising millions to fight the disease, the breast cancer movement has legitimized the wearing of pink among adult women in a way that Disney's princesses never could.

The modern pink movement began back in 1991, the year pink ribbons were distributed to all breast cancer survivors and participants in the Susan G. Komen Race for the Cure in New York City. A year later, cosmetics giant The Estée Lauder Companies, in partnership with *Self* magazine, passed out 1.5 million ribbons at its cosmetic counters. Avon followed suit with its own fund-raising crusade in 1993 and created pink-ribbon pins. The rest, as they say, is history.

Pink wasn't always so popular. Back in the 1980s, when women were first fighting their way through corporate glass ceilings, many female executives shunned pink because they felt it undermined their credibility. Pink screamed Barbie dolls and ice cream cones, instead of competent executive who deserves the same pay as her male counterpart. Many big accounting and technology firms didn't even allow women to wear the color to the office, mandating earth-tones-only policies. Well, we've come a long way, baby.

From iPods to cell phones, sneakers, and professionally licensed sports gear (even though there isn't a team out there with pink on its official uniform), pink is back. Could it be that women are finally secure enough with their place in the world to embrace the traditional color of femininity? Or is it just that the sheer number of breast cancer awareness campaigns has finally given adult women permission to wear—and buy—their favorite guilty-pleasure color?

Whether it's biology or buy-ology, one thing is for sure: October is the one month of the year when both men and women can embrace the traditional color of femininity without going pink in the cheeks.

Evolution of Pink Timeline

1955 . . . Dodge introduces pink La Femme car with matching umbrella and purse. Women just say no, and it disappears by 1957.

1962 . . . Emilio Pucci brings hot pink to the forefront of the era, introducing a haute couture collection as an homage to Jacqueline Kennedy.

1965 . . . Braniff flight attendants trade in traditional uniforms for a mod pink Pucci ensemble, complete with a stylish (and practical?) "space bubble" helmet to protect their hair.

1970s . . . Gloria Steinem popularizes the phrase "A woman needs a man like a fish needs a bicycle," and pink languishes during the second wave of the women's liberation movement.

1980 . . . Lisa Birnbach publishes *The Preppy Handbook*, and pink unites with kelly green for preppy bliss. Pink Izod Lacoste shirts become de rigueur. (Today's preppy descendants can be seen wearing the same pink/green color pairings in Lilly Pulitzer designs.)

Late 1980s . . . Pink is still no-man's-land for women who work in offices. Many major corporations and public accounting firms enact fashion policies that mandate earth tones only. Floppy maroon bow ties become ubiquitous.

1991 . . . Pink ribbons were distributed to all breast cancer survivors and participants of the Susan G. Komen Race for the Cure in New York City.

1992 . . . The Estée Lauder Companies partner with *Self* magazine to distribute 1.5 million pink ribbons at their cosmetics counters, fueling national breast cancer awareness.

1993 . . . The Avon Foundation Breast Cancer Crusade is formed in the United States and creates its own pink ribbon-shaped pins.

2001 . . . Reese Witherspoon's *Legally Blonde* character gives women everywhere the license to wear pink and be taken seriously, thanks to an unapologetically pink movie wardrobe.

2005 . . . *Pink* magazine hits the newsstands, targeting businesswomen across the United States.

2009 . . . Pink is back, but is it here to stay? Only time will tell.

Women Are the Gold Standard for Design

In classically "male" categories, women are a surprisingly great litmus test for product design.

"Women are the canaries down the coal mine when it comes to new technologies," says Genevieve Bell, PhD, a cultural anthropologist and human behavior expert for Intel, the world's leading maker of semiconductor chips. Intel's products are found in the vast majority of personal computers, and Bell has studied women and technology for more than ten years.

As we've seen with Swiffer, women want a product to work the moment it comes out of the box. They want it to be intuitive. They want it to be helpful. Bell sums it up this way: "The fact that women don't have time to configure or troubleshoot technology to me suggests that they are the gold standard for design. At some level, if you could design things that women want, everyone would want them."

Women get a bad rap when it comes to new technologies. They are often painted as the industry's laggards, while men are viewed as the early adopters. History suggests this is not true.

"Women have always been the custodians of technology in the home," says Bell. "We figured out how to make electricity work, how to use early refrigeration, early stoves, and we were in charge of the first wireless radios, telephones, sewing machines, and televisions. Women were the conduit through which new technology came into the home. But that never gets told as part of our story, because what gets celebrated is what happens in the public domain. All along, women have been the gatekeepers and fire marshals of new technology."

There are several interesting reasons women want clean, easy-to-use design, she explains. One is that women and men have different orientations toward time and different ideas about how it is best spent. In Western masculine culture, men claim bragging rights about how long it took them to do something. For instance, a man may brag, "It took me sixteen hours to digitize my CD collection this weekend." In male culture it's considered enjoyable, acceptable, and even admirable to work on complex projects for hours, and men often find these kinds of projects challenging. Before the advent of high-tech engines, one of the most common sights in America was a man bent over the engine of his car on a weekend afternoon, tinkering away.

Women can be quite the opposite in this regard. They'll say, "Oh, this outfit is something I just threw on," or "No, I don't spend much time on my hair and makeup." With so many women working two shifts—a day job and another job managing home and family—it becomes a point of pride to multitask and get things done quickly. Most women don't consider it fun or exciting to wrestle with a challenging technical issue in their free time. "There are simply too many pressures on women's time to value something that takes a lot of it," says Bell.

Women want to get to the action. If they've got a new cell phone, they want to be able to call a friend on it right away, while men may spend hours programming the phone, downloading applications, and enjoying every minute of it. This may be one of the few areas in life where men are more interested in foreplay than women.

So is feminine design just another way of saying *good* design?

Often the answer is yes. But sometimes there's an

opportunity to tap the women's market with something more.

**The Lesson of Philips:
Know what you don't know**

Myth: Entrenched "masculine" brands can't attract women in a credible way.

Reality: Yes, they can, especially when they team with brands that already do.

With the exception of Apple, the consumer electronics industry is going through an awkward kind of puberty in its attempts to appeal to women. Marrying style and technology is not easy, and adding to the complexity is the fact that there's a large contingent of women who like their electronics served up with some serious, shiny bling—crystals and other objects that look like jewelry. Young women in Asia are driving the trend, and they represent an enormous market. In places such as China and Japan, cell phones are decorated with all the drama and color of a Las Vegas showgirl. The phenomenon has created a burgeoning industry in "feminized" electronics accessories.

Royal Philips Electronics, the Dutch manufacturing giant, watched the trend grow and saw an opportunity to expand its market. The company had one obstacle to overcome. It wasn't a technology issue—Philips is a highly respected company with many inventions to its credit, including the compact disc, the audiotape cassette, the rotary electric shaver, and the first home VCR system. The issue was that historically, the company was built on an engineering heritage as masculine as a three-piece suit.

It can be tricky for any company to navigate the murky waters of feminine taste, especially one immersed in designing everything from lightbulbs and semiconductors to MRI machines. But the people at Philips were smart: they knew what they didn't know. And what they didn't know was what women wanted, so they partnered with someone who did.

"We are not a female brand," explains Nils Leseberg, the Netherlands-based director in charge of launching Philips' female-focused accessories project. "We needed to understand what it would take to create a feminine product in this area that is technologically advanced, yet very appealing to women. It became clear that we could not pull this off alone. We knew we needed to partner with someone who would bring that aspect into the whole equation."

Philips approached Swarovski, the luxury brand of crystal glass jewelry, to create a new line of electronics accessories for women. Swarovski is an established name in the global fashion world and a favorite with female celebrities.

Swarovski saw an opportunity to expand into the growing electronic accessories market, but technology was not its heritage. With so much to gain on both sides, Philips and Swarovski joined forces to "feminize" a piece of the consumer electronics industry. But which piece? Initially, they weren't sure.

MARRYING STYLE AND FUNCTION

The two corporate teams met in Paris for the first time to brainstorm. "It was like a first date," says Raymond Wong, Philips' Hong Kong–based design director for the project. "The whole time we asked ourselves, 'What do women want?'"

The combined Philips/Swarovski team decided to tackle two product categories so mundane they could be considered style vacuums: headphones for MP3 players and USB (flash) drives. From a style standpoint, these categories had nowhere to go but up, and from a functional standpoint, they were actually *wearable*.

Women dominated the project's design team, by a nose—it was a 60/40 split. The team conducted nearly thirty focus groups across the globe to get female feedback on their design ideas. The big question was how to make an elegant design that wasn't tacky. "If we were to take an everyday product like a USB drive and simply add crystals to it, that would be patronizing, and we would not be able to deliver the quality, uniqueness, and creativity that women expect," says Wong. Consequently, all the crystals that were used in this project were specially cut and developed for the new products.

Pretty and Practical, Too

The design team wanted to incorporate style that made sense—style that told a story. The end result of the team's maiden efforts for the USB drive was two feminine designs: the crystal shape of a heart, symbolizing love, and the crystal-studded shape of a lock, symbolizing security. The MP3 headphones, meanwhile, looked like diamond earrings in a teardrop shape. "We discovered in our focus groups that women view these headphones as practical, day-to-day objects," says Wong. "They wanted to have a sparkle from a distance, but attention to detail and richness when they looked at the product close up."

Style and performance were just two parts of a larger

context that the design team took into consideration. The companies studied the broader environment in which women would handle and store these objects. In particular, they studied the role of the purse. It's a fact of life that women store just about everything in their purses, and they're always losing or destroying things at the bottom of them. "This is one of the reasons the USB lock was specially designed to hang on the outside of a purse," said Wong. "It's a beautiful accent to the bag, and it's practical. Whereas if you were to design a USB stick for a man, you'd make it flat and compact, so he could put it in his pocket."

BUSINESS UNUSUAL FOR PHILIPS

The product line was launched with glamorous events, including a fashion show in Beijing and a sneak preview at the famous Colette boutique in Paris. From the beginning, both Philips and Swarovski positioned Active Crystals as a luxury product line, sold primarily at Swarovski boutiques, as well as online. Where you *won't* find them is in most so-called big-box electronic retailers. This has been a deliberate strategy, according to Philips, which didn't want Active Crystals to get lost in an environment in which a woman wouldn't be in the right frame of mind to buy a fashion item. After all, if a woman stopped by a traditional electronics retailer to to buy toner for a printer and ran across Active Crystals on the shelf next to it, she might not be open to viewing them as the luxury products they are. It would be a case of wrong place, wrong time.

Philips says this is just the beginning of its female-focused endeavors. "We believe there are other categories in consumer electronics that are very appealing to women that haven't been tapped yet with a real fusion of design and technology," says Leseberg. "The women's opportunity needs a long-term vision and a long-term view in order to grow to the size that it can be."

There are several instructive takeaways from the Active Crystals story:

1. **If your company doesn't have brand credentials with women, consider partnering with one that does, at least for your maiden efforts.**

2. **Include women on your product development teams.**
   At the risk of stating the obvious, their insights are invaluable and can help ensure that important details aren't missed, such as understanding how women use their purses for storage.

3. **Determine whether your existing distribution channels are appropriate for a feminized new product line.**
   You may have an opportunity to expand into new channels, as Philips did with Swarovski boutiques.

More than five years after the inception of the Active Crystals project, there is no longer an active partnership between Philips and Swarovski, but it is not for lack of success. Both companies were able to glean insights for new, women-focused products in their own industries, and they remain in contact should the opportunity for a similar project arise.

Philips and Venus both represent *overt* approaches to the women's market. But far more common is the *covert* approach, in which a company creates its products to appeal to women in a way that is so subtle, neither men nor women are conscious that women are the target.

> ### The Lesson of Ryland Homes:
> ### If the woman doesn't want it,
> ### the man doesn't get it

Myth: Men drive all the big decisions in married
households.
Reality: Women are the deal breakers.

You'd be hard-pressed to find an industry more male-
dominated than home building. The average home-building
company is staffed like a World War II aircraft carrier, at
least in its management ranks. But times are slowly changing. While most senior executives are still white and male,
these companies are waking to the fact that their real customers are women, and that they've been leaving money
on the table by creating and selling homes from a male
perspective, from underdesigning closets to using sell
sheets that focus purely on technical data and architectural
blueprints.

The Ryland Group is a $2 billion, publicly traded home-
building company—one of the top in its industry—that
has changed the way it designs houses, based on a new
understanding of who rules America's roosts. In one of
the world's biggest housing downturns, the company is
leveraging its knowledge of the alpha consumer every way
it can.

If you've never thought of a home as a product before,
think again—a new home is the ultimate consumer lifestyle
product. For most people, there is no bigger purchase, literally or figuratively. As is the case with all major consumer-
product categories, women dominate.

"Women influence 91 percent of new home purchases,"

says Eric Elder, the senior executive who has championed most of Ryland's female-focused efforts. For several years now, single women have been the fastest-growing segment of the home-buying market, buying twice as many homes as single men. I worked with Ryland on a two-year research project to understand what women want in a new home. As a result, the company implemented a variety of covert, female-friendly efforts across the company. The goal was to make these changes imperceptible to home buyers, so that women would feel drawn to Ryland's homes but men would not feel excluded.

Designing Women

As discussed in Chapter 3, when a woman goes off to the workforce, she changes her personal traffic patterns, along with those of everyone in her family. As such, working mothers were the biggest catalyst for modifying Ryland's floor plans. The company redesigned the common areas of many of its models so that multitasking moms could keep one eye on the kids and one eye on the stove. Windows were built over kitchen sinks to provide a direct line of sight to the backyard. Open kitchen/family room layouts were designed with nooks for desks, so that kids could do their homework on the computer or watch TV while Mom looked on from nearby. These designs were an acknowledgment of the "time compression" that occurs within families when both parents work. Instead of parents spending an hour or two helping kids with homework and then making dinner, both activities are now likely to happen at the same time.

Time compression and the blurring of boundaries between work and home means that home isn't quite the sanctuary it once was. With cell phones, mobile devices, laptops, and the Internet, work is "part of the furniture" at home, too. In an effort to replace what's been lost, Ryland redesigned its master bedrooms as oases for stress relief. New master suites were designed as retreats for the adults in the house—and in particular, women. "A private, relaxing, reenergizing space is especially important to single mothers, who don't get much time on their own," says Elder. Many of Ryland's master bedroom suites now feature a coffee bar, mini fridge, and lounge area.

WELCOME TO THE NEIGHBORHOOD

Modifications to Ryland's floor plans were just the beginning. The company also embarked on design changes to its neighborhoods. It learned that women don't view themselves as buying just a house with four walls; they feel like they're buying an entire community, a neighborhood, a school district, and a lifestyle. Women believe a new house is going to improve their life, along with the lives of everyone in their family. If it won't, they might as well stay where they are. Subsequently, Ryland began creating more female-friendly amenities in its neighborhood designs, including cul-de-sacs, better street lighting, pocket parks, electronic garage doors as a standard feature, better lighting around home entryways, and secure gated entries in townhouse communities.

Embracing Personalization

As part of the female-friendly process, Ryland completely overhauled its design centers, the places where customers pick out their options and upgrades after signing a contract for a new home. These centers had a history of being housed in the bare garages of model homes.

"In our industry, picking out home options and upgrades used to be a back-office function," says Elder. "We'd have a hodgepodge of display cases given to us by random suppliers, with a few samples of products here and there, bad lighting . . . the whole experience was an afterthought." It couldn't be more different now. "We actually embrace the personalization process, when we used to fight it," explains Elder. "It's one of the biggest changes that's occurred at the company, and it's wholly driven by women." A senior female executive at Ryland, Diane Morrison, was the force behind the company's new design centers. She recognized that for many women, the appointment at the design center is the most exciting part of the home-buying process: it is here that they get to pick out all the things that will make the home distinctly their own.

Ryland also broadened the color palettes on its home exteriors, to help women feel that their new home has a unique, personal identity, and to diminish the dreaded "cookie cutter" effect. Instead of offering three exterior colors in a one-hundred-house community, Ryland now typically offers from nine to fifteen.

LESSONS FROM THE COVERT APPROACH

Ryland is a great example of a masculine industry that's responded to women with subtle design changes that benefit both sexes.

"Every architect that's designed homes throughout the history of this company has been a man," says Elder. "Closets used to be leftover spaces that were essentially a door and a hole. Now they are a design element of the home, with functionality built into them. Our sales lobbies, which used to be fairly bare, now have places to sit down, with inspirational reading materials, like home design magazines, and toys for kids. And we've changed our merchandising displays so that they are more emotionally charged and filled with pictures of people."

When the covert approach is done right, men don't even notice the design elements that have been added for women. It turns out that men like the idea of having a hot cup of coffee in their master bedroom, too. "From a consumer standpoint, men would live in the garage if they had to," says Elder with a grin. "Women want the home, and men want the women to get what they want. The great thing for us is that the changes we've made have been driven by women but are appreciated by men, too."

When you appeal to women in a covert fashion, the men find themselves on the receiving end of things they never knew they wanted but are happy to get—and maybe even pay more for the next time. The lesson is this: when you make women happy, you make everyone happy. Women are the leading economic indicators of what people want. Key learnings from Ryland include:

1. **Never underestimate the influence of women in a "couples" purchase.**

   Women are the veto vote for buying decisions large and small, from deciding what home to buy to where to eat. The individual who conducts the financial transaction (which can often be the husband) is not always the primary decision maker. If you sell to a lot of couples, figure out the "hot buttons" for both your male and female customers. They may be very different.

2. **Study how the divorce rate and the increased spending power of single women may be impacting your industry.**

   The phenomenon can open new opportunities in product design, as it did with Ryland and its master bedroom retreats, and also in the services that support your product offerings.

3. **A well-crafted, subtle approach attracts women and pleases men, too.**

   It's socially unacceptable for men to buy products that are overtly feminine. By being subtle in your appeal to women—through a covert approach—you have the ability to attract both sexes without alienating either one. Married women never want to see their husbands alienated or emasculated. (Not if they're happily married, anyway.)

Covert Success Stories

FROM houses to cleaning products to household appliances and a good bottle of wine, a covert approach can broaden markets and build revenue.

Dutch Boy, a major paint brand from Sherwin-Williams, revolutionized the paint industry by creating easy-to-open Twist & Pour containers that allow people to pour paint in essentially the same way they pour liquid laundry detergent—from a plastic container with a handle and screw-top cap. The company realized that no one, particularly women, enjoys dealing with the traditional metal paint can lids that need to be opened and closed with screwdrivers and are notoriously difficult to pour without spilling.

"Eighty-six percent of the time, [paint] color is either selected by the female or she's the major influencer," says Adam Chafe, a Dutch Boy senior executive. "If you know who's making the decisions, that's where you get your insights." Creating an entirely new paint container was no small undertaking for Dutch Boy. The company had to retrofit tens of thousands of paint shakers in retail locations, because they were literally trying to fit a square peg (the new design for Twist & Pour is a square) into a round hole. It also had to retool the company's plants, which were created for metal cans. Sherwin-Williams continues to innovate based on consumer insights, and in 2008 launched Refresh by Dutch Boy, a line of paint that absorbs odors out of the air, created in partnership with Arm & Hammer. "Odor management is completely female-driven," says Chafe. "Frankly, men care a lot less about how a home smells than women do."

Women may drive the do-it-yourself industry—especially when it comes to interior design changes—yet the Twist & Pour and Refresh lines are products that men can appreciate, too.

Whirlpool, a client I worked with for years and one of the world's leading appliance manufacturers, introduced its successful Duet European-style front-loading washing machines to a country of women who hate to bend and squat (America, this means us). The Duet features pedestals in 10- and 15.5-inch heights that raise the washer and dryer for comfortable loading and less bending, and incorporates a sophisticated "bubble" design for its doors that make homeowners of both sexes proud to show off the products, instead of wanting to hide them in the basement or laundry room.

Red Bicyclette, the French wine from the American E. & J. Gallo Winery, has been a major success for the winemaking giant. The label features a whimsical, cute-as-a-*bouton* cartoon of a Frenchman in a beret riding a red bike, with a dog running behind him holding a baguette in its mouth. Gallo has created a nonintimidating, cleverly marketed French wine for a new generation of brand-obsessed consumers. With a website laden with recipes and headlines such as "You Grow, Grapes!" Gallo clearly had women in its crosshairs when it created the brand, but its label is subtle enough for men. Hold on to your berets—but in the short time since its 2004 introduction, Red Bicyclette has become the number one premium French wine sold in the United States.

The Lesson of Callaway:
Women can revitalize flat industries

Myth: There are just some things, like golf, that will
always be a man's game.

Reality: Given the right equipment and a welcoming
environment, women will not only get involved,
they'll bring the next generation with them.

Targeting women with a sex-specific product has the potential to shift an entire industry. That's what one company is
hoping will happen with golf, that bastion of (white) male
power and prestige. The number of golf rounds played has
been flat since 2005. The game's player pool has shrunk 7
percent over the last five years.[6] Many in the industry think
the only way to grow the sport is to get more people into it.
Who might these people be? You guessed it—women.

The obstacles are many. One is the matter of time. Few
people under retirement age can regularly take a day off to
play eighteen holes of golf. In our blink-and-you-missed-it
world, it now feels like too much time away from the office
or the family (or the cell phone). Golf is still a costly sport,
and at many courses both the price and intimidation factor
are enough to keep newcomers away. In some places, the
snobbish golf environment spoofed in the movie *Caddy-
shack* still exists (except it's not nearly as funny). Even now,
women who wander into pro shops get asked if they're lost,
and sometimes they have a hard time getting good tee times
because the premium slots are saved for men. Discrimina-
tion against women at golf clubs still exists. The Augusta National Golf Club in Georgia, for example, is one of the most
revered courses in the sport—the setting of the Masters

tournament each year—and yet it still does not allow women as members. Here's a story from an avid golfer in her late thirties, named Sarah, who lives in Indianapolis.

> *There used to be a group of women at my club who would play bridge out on the terrace. One day they overheard some men using a lot of profanity on the course. The women complained to the manager about the language they'd heard. What was the club's response? The next day they put a sign up saying that bridge would no longer be allowed on the terrace.*

On paper, there's no reason golf shouldn't be wildly popular with women. The sport requires finesse instead of brute strength. It's social. It's peaceful. It's played in the most beautiful settings imaginable. It's coed. The fashion is great. Cocktails and conversation await at the end of every game. Yet women make up a paltry 25 percent or less of all golfers in the United States, which is one of the reasons the game is stagnating. Golf equipment manufacturer Callaway is one company that believes offering women the right products might get more of them onto the greens and revitalize an industry that's hit a growth plateau. We know that women have the balls to play golf. But do they have the clubs?

That's where Callaway comes in.

AN INDUSTRY OUTSIDER BRINGS A NEW VISION TO THE SPORT

Callaway Golf makes the Big Bertha, one of the world's most famous clubs. The company is a leader in the golf equipment industry, and Callaway's CEO, George Fellows, has a deep knowledge of women consumers—unusual for a golf executive—because he's the former CEO of Revlon. When Fellows arrived at Callaway in 2005, he saw an opportunity so large it was nearly blinding: get more women into the game and grow the game itself.

"It was a glaring opening," says Fellows. "Women were being ill-served." As the father of two daughters, Fellows has long advocated for women's participation in all aspects of sports, business, and life. He's concerned that women see golf as an exclusionary sport, and he wants to help change those perceptions by creating more products for the other half.

"For some reason, our society still hasn't caught up to the fact that women should participate at the exact same levels as men in a whole host of activities, but in order to do that appropriately, they've got to be equipped in the right way," says Fellows.

When golfers are saddled with ill-fitting equipment, they don't hit the ball as well, and therefore don't feel confident out on the course—which subsequently keeps them off it. Women have long been at a historical disadvantage in the sport, because "women's clubs were largely men's clubs with pink shafts," says Fellows.

The opportunity thus identified, Fellows and his team embarked on creating new clubs for Callaway's Gems line, to accommodate the physical differences of women. Instead of tweaking men's clubs, Callaway specifically designed the Gems line for women's bodies.

SWING LIKE A GIRL

Based on input from women golfers, instructors, and designers, the clubs are engineered with female-specific ergonomic adaptations for head design, head size, swing weight, shaft weight, shaft flexibility, and grip size.

By enabling women to hit the ball better, Callaway hopes the Gems line will increase women's confidence and reduce the intimidation factor that keeps many out of the game.

Callaway has women on its product development team, and a woman heads up marketing for the Gems line. "There's nothing worse than having a bunch of men trying to decide what women would prefer," laughs Fellows. "We do what any other consumer-products company would do. We show our product to our target market, and we ask them what they think."

Experience is on Fellows' side. As a former "lipstick" guy, he understands women's shopping patterns better than most of his peers in the golf industry, or any other industry, for that matter. And although he doesn't have control over the way golf courses are run, he and his team evangelize to the people who do about the opportunity women provide for the industry.

"Women represent a more robust financial model because they spend more money than men," he explains. "Some of that spending happens to be in fashion and the other accoutrements of playing golf, but why does that matter? It just makes them a more attractive target."

WOMEN: GATEKEEPERS TO THE NEXT GENERATION

Women are also critical to bringing in another target audience: the next generation of golfers. This is because when women get involved in an activity, their families follow. Golf is one of the few sports in which the whole family could spend an entire day playing together, as opposed to most other sports, in which parents must sit patiently (or possibly impatiently) in the stands watching their kids. And since people have smaller families these days, it's easier to accommodate an entire family in just one golf cart.

"If you've got the mother, the father, and the kids participating in a game of golf on the weekend, time is no longer an issue," says Fellows. Quite the contrary: time now becomes a friend, because it provides an opportunity for family togetherness in a beautiful outdoor setting. "It's absurd that we as an industry are not doing more to promote this," says Fellows. "Then instead of golf rounds being flat, you'd see them grow."

Fellows' formula is clearly working for Callaway. The company finished 2008 with the second-highest sales level in the company history.[7] Callaway's board of directors voted to extend Fellows' employment as CEO, based on the company's exceptional performance. Whether the rest of the golf industry—the people who run the courses and clubs—takes advantage of the opportunity remains to be seen.

Key learnings from the Callaway story include:

1. **Women can help grow a flat industry.**

   If you're in a product category or industry that's hit a plateau, focusing on women may help bring in new customers and revenues.

2. **Women are key to the next generation of customers.**

   If you want children and teenagers to participate in an activity, get their mothers excited about it.

3. **Women's participation has a multiplier effect in terms of people and purchases.**

Not only do women bring their friends and family members to companies and activities that they're thrilled with, they spend money differently, and often more of it, on the accoutrements.

Success Stories from Overt Strategies

SOME exceptional companies have transformed unisex products to specifically target women. The phrase "game changer" is overused, but in Nintendo's case, it's accurate. From the moment of its introduction in 2006, the Nintendo Wii broadened the audience for gaming, specifically targeting moms and women of all ages with its new system. It effectively tapped into a market most of the gaming industry had long ignored, with the notable exception of the Sims franchise from Electronic Arts, which has long been a female favorite. Nintendo's efforts have taken root fast. As we've seen, 40 percent of gamers in the United States are now female, and 50 percent of the Wii's purchasers are women.[8] With Wii Fit, the follow-up product that Nintendo introduced in May 2008, the company continues to attract women in droves, and as of this writing, the product is poised to overtake one of the world's most iconically male video games, Grand Theft Auto, in sales.[9]

The Nintendo Wii does so many things well that it's hard to narrow them down, but the effort deserves a try. First, the company promotes the fact that all members of the family can take advantage of the game's wide range of activities, which is smart because women are interested in how other members of the household will be affected by the products they buy. Second, it shows normal-looking people in its advertising, making the product approachable and unintimidating. Finally, it actively promotes the fact that Nintendo wants women as players, through its overtly female-focused "play dates" and promotions at women-centric conferences and events. As Nintendo North America president Reggie Fils-Aime remarked to a reporter from the *Los Angeles Times,* "We're seeing demand from a whole new market. Of the people who stood in line [for Wii Fit] in New York, 60 percent were working women. This is a demo that arguably has never bought a video game, and they're buying it for themselves."[10]

All that Wii playing requires a lot of energy, which brings us to another category: food. The Luna brand of whole-nutrition energy bars for women has become one of the top-selling brands in the category in the United States. Created by privately held Clif Bar & Company, Luna was designed for women's specific nutritional needs, and the brand represents the growing trend of food products created just for women. In fact, the burgeoning category of so-called functional foods has found a responsive audience in women, especially in the forty-plus age group. From products such as Activia yogurt from Dannon (which aids digestion) to the countless orange juice brands and other beverages promoting calcium as an ingredient, food manufacturers are capitalizing on women's innate interest in health and well-being by marketing products just for them.

Women are also tearing down the dingy drywall of the home-improvement industry, adding color, style, and revenue to this traditionally male-dominated realm. Firms such as Barbara K Enterprises, Tomboy Tools, and Girlgear Industries have reinvented everything from power tools to hammers, toolboxes, and tool belts. The redesigned products have been created with women's anatomy in mind (the tools are easier to grip, hold, and lift) as well as women's style considerations (the products feature bright colors and sleek designs).

Creating products for women isn't about sacrificing one gender to gain the business of another. Ideally, it's about broadening your reach and increasing your revenues by adding more products that appeal to the world's primary shoppers. Once you've got the product right, the next critical step comes into play: making women want it.

5

MARKETING

TO WOMEN

The Difference Between Sex Appeal
and Gender Appeal

What do women want?
Don Draper, creative director, Sterling Cooper Advertising
Who cares?
Roger Sterling, partner, Sterling Cooper Advertising
—From season one of the AMC drama *Mad Men,*
set in a fictional ad agency in 1960

Marketing, and especially advertising, its most glamorous representation, is the public arena in which a company's insights about women—or lack thereof—are most vividly on display.

We already know that women buy the vast majority of consumer products. What's less well known is that more than 90 percent of U.S. ad agency creative directors are men, and the majority of top chief marketing officers (nearly 70 percent) are men, too.[1] At many agencies, the creative department is like a boys' club, complete with foosball table.

Campaigns that are meant for women often end up being filtered through the eyes of men, and sometimes things get lost in translation. Not always, of course—there are incredibly talented men working in marketing. But one has to wonder, in an economy in which women dominate consumer spending so thoroughly, what if the tables were turned? What if 90 percent of the world's creative directors were women instead of men? Would marketing look different? Would sales results look different? My guess is that they would. And it does beg the question of why, nearly fifty years after the setting of the television series *Mad Men,* which focuses on the lives of employees in a male-dominated ad agency, the creative department still so often looks like something out of the Eisenhower administration.

I don't have the answers to these questions, but I do know that no matter how complex the marketing function becomes or how cluttered the media environment is, there are still only two sexes on the receiving end of a marketing message. Understanding the one that does most of the buying is crucial, especially when there's such a big difference between gender appeal and sex appeal.

Gender appeal is the type of marketing that resonates strongly with the culture of a particular sex. Its messages and images tap into a gender's collective consciousness—its rites of passage, milestones, communication styles, body issues, desires, and motivations. The pain of adolescence is universal, for example, but the memories and feelings associated with a first period are very specific to women, just as the memories of a first (public) erection are very specific to men. Yet people overlook gender the way they overlook oxygen, which is a mistake, since we now know that gender is one of the primary filters through which people understand and interpret life.

Sex appeal is different—it defines words, images, or people that others find arousing. And when it comes to being aroused, most of us have lived long enough to know that women and men have different ideas about what's sexy and what's not.

Right now I'm staring at a poster for Rémy Martin cognac. It features two gorgeous women in a provocative embrace. An imaginary wind blows through their hair. One woman has the other woman's necklace in her mouth and is clenching it with her teeth. It looks like something wild is about to happen between them. The tagline reads, "Things are getting interesting." The ad stops me in my tracks. Its implication is that men who order Rémy Martin may be rewarded for their choice by seeing two beautiful women get it on. What a way to sell cognac! I can't help laughing when I realize this ad is so thoroughly steeped in male culture, it could never work in reverse.

Imagine it: a similar ad targeting women, featuring two scantily clad men in a provocative pose, with one of them clenching the other man's jewelry in his teeth. Ludicrous! It's safe to say that not only would women laugh at the ad, they'd assume it was targeted to gay men. The Rémy Martin ad, like so many others similar to it, demonstrates the gender canyon between what men and women fantasize about, what they aspire to, and what motivates them to choose a product. Understanding this difference between gender appeal and sex appeal is one of the most fundamental principles in marketing to women.

Luckily for men, a woman's brain is much less interested

in how a man looks than in how he thinks and acts.[2] Research has proven what we all know from experience—that men devote much more time to thinking about sex than women do. "When asked to think of nothing, women are thinking about relationships, while men are thinking about sports or sex," confirms Dr. Daniel Amen, the brain-imaging expert and author of *Sex on the Brain.* With so many male creative directors, is it any wonder that advertising is filled with such an astounding number of sexualized images of women—not to mention sports references?

Every marketer knows that the most effective campaigns create an emotional connection with audiences. But what if one audience has an entirely different emotional reality than the other? As we have seen throughout this book, women have different emotional perceptions, responses, and memories than men do. When these differences aren't understood well enough, campaigns fail to connect with their targets. They become instantly forgettable, which is why the world is littered with campaigns that most of us couldn't recall at gunpoint. The good news is this: armed with the right knowledge, both men and women can learn to create marketing campaigns with gender appeal.

What's Hot and What's Not: It's Different for Women

FOR an entertaining example of gender appeal, check out the photo book series *Porn for Women,* which is a spoof on the qualities women find sexy in men.[3] The books feature pictures of handsome, fully clothed men performing mundane household tasks and complimenting an unseen woman—

the reader—in ways that women fantasize about. The books are filled with images of men staring into the camera and saying things like "Antiquing makes me *hot!*" "I'm so excited for your sister to have her baby!" and "Hey, guess what? I just paid off the mortgage!" The books possess off-the-charts gender appeal, because hearing these kinds of phrases is a genuine fantasy for many women. There's even a great new word, *choreplay,* that describes the happiness and fuzzy glow that women get when men pitch in with the household chores.

While *Porn for Women* is clearly satire, it's a great example of how women's and men's fantasies can be so different. And because so much of marketing is about tapping into people's fantasies of being more beautiful, successful, and happy, understanding that there are differences in how each gender defines what it means to be any of these things is critical.

For MasterCard, a Good Story Is Priceless When Marketing to Women

MASTERCARD Worldwide and the team of people at its ad agency, McCann-Erickson Worldwide, provide a superb example of how one company has mastered the art of gender appeal.

The "Priceless" campaign has leapt over the walls of marketing and made its way into pop culture. It appears in 110 countries and fifty-one languages and has been running since 1997. The campaign is worth studying for many reasons, but for our purposes, it's because the folks at Master-Card have perfected the art of emotionally connecting to the world's most powerful spenders (women) while still retaining the brand's appeal with men—not so simple in a sector of the financial industry that has all the warmth of sheet metal.

"Priceless" ads tell small but perfectly formed stories about all the things in life that money can't buy.

"The campaign is deceptively simple, " says Amy Fuller, who runs marketing for MasterCard in the Americas. "But it's unbelievably difficult to find the human insights that becomes the content for the (television) spots." Amy has one of those jobs that everyone thinks they can do. Perfect strangers give her their ideas for "Priceless" commercials when they find out what she does for a living, because MasterCard makes storytelling look easy, the way Tiger Woods makes golf look easy.

The details are what's different

Universal needs such as love, time, family, and children are all considered priceless by most people, but these generalities don't necessarily make for compelling marketing, because there's nothing surprising about them. The details are what this campaign does well. The "Priceless" commercials depict life's golden moments through the seemingly insignificant things that make up our days, like a ready-made lasagna; a pedicure; a rubber ball; or a box of Goobers candy. It's the specifics in the campaign that make women think, *They're talking to me—that's my life.*

Time after time, MasterCard displays a fundamental understanding of female psychology. For one thing, the campaign's creators clearly know that women rationalize their purchases, especially when spending money on themselves.

(Men just don't seem to have the same guilt gene that women do.) In one of my favorite executions, a commercial called "That Would Go Great with That," MasterCard demonstrates how one small purchase has the domino effect of leading to bigger and bigger ones. In the commercial, which features a woman who could be described as lovely but not unattainably beautiful, every new purchase the woman makes is justified by the previous one. Take a look at the copy, which is read to great effect on television by the campaign's regular male announcer for U.S. ads, actor Billy Crudup.

Pedicure . . . $28 on debit MasterCard.
Peep-toe pumps to show off your pedicure . . . $96 on
debit card.
Adorable dress, to go with your peep-toe pumps that
show off your pedicure . . . $150 on debit card.

Cut to a screen shot of the woman admiring a beautiful necklace in the window of Tiffany's, until the voice-over says, "Yeah, right." She rolls her eyes, smiles, and skips away, laughing at herself for thinking she could justify expensive new jewelry just because she got a good pedicure. She had gotten carried away.

The voice-over closes with: "Living in the moment, priceless. There are some things money can't buy. For everything you must have right now, there's debit MasterCard."

The insight of this ad is that MasterCard understands how women shop. Women don't have a linear purchasing style; rather, the act of buying one small thing can snowball into a series of unplanned purchases. Interestingly, a woman creative director has run the "Priceless" campaign since its inception. Her name is Joyce King Thomas, and she's still with the campaign's original agency, McCann Erickson.

"Both men and women like the campaign because we take things to a human place," says King Thomas. "If you can find some big human truth, it's always better than a purely functional message. The two pieces of this campaign are head and heart. We start with the functional benefit—that you can use your card to buy these things—but we know that there's more to life than money, and that people want experiences, and something more soulful. Women respond to that, but we also have big, burly men cry when we test commercials." Joyce is that rare bird, a female creative director at a big New York ad agency. Is it a coincidence that a woman has led one of the world's most successful and longest-running campaigns? You already know what I think.

How MasterCard avoids alienating men

Credit card penetration is evenly split between men and women, so like most businesses, MasterCard can't afford to alienate men. Women are bigger debit card users and buy the vast majority of consumer products. So the company develops creative treatments based on the audience of the vehicles in which the ads appear—a male focus for men's magazines, a female focus for women's magazines, and so on. In its general-market advertising, MasterCard is adept at addressing the milestones and life stages that are common to both men and women, such as the moment a couple's kids go off to college. On the surface, these ads appeal to both sexes, but under the surface, they appeal strongly to female psychology. Women are typically in charge of life's milestones—the birthdays, the graduations, the celebrations—and thus the ads speak particularly loudly to them, in a way that may be imperceptible to men. Even when MasterCard uses a male star, such as professional football player Peyton Manning, "we show him vulnerable and we let him be a person," says King Thomas.

Priceless lessons for your business

Key takeaways from MasterCard include:

- **Storytelling is one of the most powerful techniques for creating an emotional connection with women.**
The oldest form of communication is still the best.

- **Ideas centered on the human experience are the ones that translate most easily around the world.**
If you're embarking on a global campaign, MasterCard offers a textbook example of localized executions created under universal human truths.

- **Give a campaign both a head and a heart.**
Women respond to personal experiences and examples more than they do to product specifications. If it's women you're after, make them the heroes, not the product.

Gender Appeal Means Showing Some Personality: Just ask the People at method

BY now you may be thinking, *What about smaller companies that don't have a tenth of the budget of MasterCard and will likely never produce a national broadcast campaign, let alone an international one?*

Consider this marketing strategy: *stand for something.* It's a wonderful philosophy for any business, and it's especially effective for small ones. Small brands need big personalities. They need a point of view. One of women's core motivators is connecting with other people. If you develop a personality that invites women to connect with your brand based on a shared point of view or shared values, then you've really got gender appeal.

For inspiration, look no further than the category-disrupting entrepreneurs at the helm of method Inc., based in San Francisco. method produces high-design, great-smelling, ecofriendly household cleaning products that people display in their homes like artwork. It's elevated humble soaps and cleansers to a level of hipness once reserved only for designer jeans. The products (which cost just a few dollars) come in containers with beautiful and aesthetically pleasing shapes, like soap bottles that look like post-modern bowling pins. But the brand is more than just good looks: it stands for something. Gorgeous with a worldview, method is quite possibly the Angelina Jolie of the house-cleaning aisle. That's because method's founders view their company as a cause, and they market it that way.

Though it's now a $100 million firm with 150 products, the company was founded by two childhood best friends, Eric Ryan and Adam Lowry, in the year 2000, when they were both still in their twenties. Ryan and Lowry had the idea of infusing design and ecofriendliness into the cleaning products category, the dullest aisle in the grocery store. But their bigger idea was to create nothing short of a revolution against dirt.

"A great company doesn't start a company, it starts a cause," declares the charismatic Ryan. "Our cause at method is getting a bunch of dirty things out of the world. We think of our brand as a movement."

Spend a few minutes with Ryan and you'll walk away feeling like you, too, want to change the world, and are slightly ashamed that you haven't—yet.

Most entrepreneurs start a business based on something they love. Not these guys. Ryan hated to clean. His bedroom was a mess. He knew he wasn't alone. "Our big insight was that your home is a very high-interest, high-emotion place, and even though people don't love cleaning, they do love home design, and they take a lot of pride in their home," he says. "We thought that if we connected the love and emotion of your home with the products that you need to care for it, we would probably have the basis for a business. It's like what Williams-Sonoma did by focusing on the joy of cooking, not the chore of cooking."

Ryan and Lowry felt strongly about creating an eco-friendly business. They thought it was ironic that chemicals with skulls and crossbones on the labels were used to clean the most sacred space in the world: your home. "Why are we using poison to make our homes healthier? This stuff should actually be good for you," says Ryan. And that's how the idea for method was born.

People against dirty

method developed a philosophy of environmentally friendly design through every aspect of its business, and then built the entire brand around it. The company created a manifesto that has culminated in a witty grassroots marketing campaign called "People Against Dirty: Dedicated to the Fight Against Dirty, in Whatever Form it Appears." method's definition of dirty is broad, encompassing everything from animal cruelty to poor indoor air quality.

The big idea is that by buying its products, method's customers can join the company's fight to rid the world of toxins and ugly chemicals inside the home, and everywhere else, too. There is a "People Against Dirty" blog. There are fan sites. There are advocates. method's customers are pre-dominantly women, and many feel like they're making a statement about themselves every time they put one of the company's pretty bottles next to a faucet. The products say, *Not only do I have great taste, I am also ecofriendly.*

"We think of our customers as people against dirty, and we think of ourselves as people against dirty," says Ryan. "Essentially we think of our customers as an advocacy group." method treats its most vocal customers as public relations conduits. The company sends them the same press kits and samples it sends to traditional journalists. These customers then blog about the products, and voilà—method pops up over and over again in all the social media everyone else is chasing.

Your budget can be small if you're willing to think big

method didn't use a big marketing budget to put itself on the map, mainly because it didn't have one. The "People Against Dirty" manifesto captured the imagination of the press and the public. It was the right message at the right time—the environmental movement was just gaining steam in the United States. The combination of a strong, eco-friendly philosophy and high style proved to be a recipe for generating truckloads of publicity.

Ryan and Lowry felt so passionate about style and its potential as a marketing tool that they were able to persuade world-class industrial designer Karim Rashid—who is known for creating award-winning products for companies such as Umbra—to create a modern, clean, understated design for the new line. From day one, the products generated media coverage in women's magazines, on television shows, and on websites. "I believed from the beginning that our packaging could be a marketing vehicle," says Ryan, who was a marketer himself before founding method.

The company has now expanded into the United Kingdom, Canada, and Australia and is creating distribution relationships in other countries. It recently broadened its product offerings by introducing personal-care products for babies, calling the line "Squeaky Clean Baby." With these new products, method has cleverly leveraged the credibility it has with women and extended it into a line they will buy for their children.

If you're part of a smaller company with a tight marketing budget, it's worth asking a few questions: What do you stand for? What do you stand against? When a woman buys your product, what does that say about her? How can you align yourself with an idea bigger than the product itself? How can you make a woman feel smarter simply by using your product or service? The exercise just might lead you to a more refined positioning that women can connect with. Women are always looking for what they have in common with someone else. What does she have in common with you?

Key takeaways from method are:

- **If you've got a small brand, give it a big personality.**
When you're up against major spenders, an outsized personality helps you compete against outsized budgets.

- **Align your brand with a bigger idea.**
method elevated the idea of household cleaning into a campaign to rid the world of dirty things. Is there a bigger idea you can wrap around your brand?

- **Challenge yourself from a design standpoint.**
Pretend you're from an entirely different industry when looking at your design and packaging. If you worked at BMW, how might you approach the design of your product? Can you bring in fresh industrial design resources? Packaging has the power to shake up commoditized industries. method did it. Altoids did it. Dutch Boy did it. Kleenex did it. Maybe you can, too.

Bluefly Masters the Sweet Spot: Integrating Online and Offline Marketing

HOW often do you watch TV while tapping on your laptop or mobile phone? If your answer is "a lot," you're not alone.

Research about Internet use makes it clear that most people multitask. More than 80 percent of people online are involved with another medium, activity, or device at the same time they're on their computers.[4] Most often that medium is television. And when it comes to integrating TV with the Internet, few people have done it better than the folks behind the partnership of online fashion retailer Bluefly.com and the Bravo network's *Project Runway*. (The show has since moved to Lifetime.) In the parlance of its viewers, this partnership was the ultimate hookup.

The *Project Runway* reality show pits up-and-coming fashion designers in a contest to be anointed as the next big thing. Hosted by supermodel Heidi Klum and featuring fashion heavyweights as judges, the show decides the fate of aspiring designers by pronouncing who's in and who's out at the end of every episode. The winner gets $100,000 to start his or her own line of fashion clothing.

Bluefly teamed up with the show during its fourth and fifth seasons, and brought *Project Runway* to life by integrating its products into the show so seamlessly that it effectively became a player in the drama. How Bluefly did this is a veritable primer on integrated marketing.

First, Bluefly cleverly made available for purchase (on its website) the styles featured on every episode. Viewers didn't have to passively watch all the fashions paraded before them—they could buy close approximations of each designer's styles by 6:30 a.m. on the site the morning after each show. "We knew that everyone was talking about *Project Runway* on Thursday mornings, so we wanted to send them to Bluefly," says Melissa Payner, the retailer's CEO. The theme of the promotion was "Bluefly and *Project Runway:* Shop What Happened."

A key part of the promotion was Bluefly's sponsorship of the highly promoted "Accessories Wall" in the design contestants' workroom, showcasing bags, jewelry, and shoes the designers could use to accompany their designs. The Bluefly name was mentioned several times each episode, usually by the show's design mentor, Tim Gunn. In an accompanying feature on Bluefly called "Off the Wall," viewers could then buy the same accessories featured on the wall in the show. By allowing visitors to "shop what happened," Bluefly effectively transformed its inventory into a story. The outfits Bluefly featured were now more than just clothes—they were part of the excitement of *Project Runway*.

The retailer also made itself an integral part of the winner's prize. *Project Runway* heavily promoted the fact that the winning designer had the opportunity to sell their new collection on Bluefly. It also offered a $10,000 shopping spree on its site for a winning viewer. "Our traffic would spike the same moment Tim Gunn would mention the shopping spree," says Payner. As a way to more closely link itself to the show, Bluefly's website featured a charming blog by its merchandising coordinator, Mindy Dorf, who shared what it was like to be behind the scenes of the show. She wrote it with all the gushing enthusiasm you'd expect of a young fan. Through everything it did, Bluefly positioned itself as just that—a fan that was as crazy about the show as its customers were.

Bluefly created a shared experience with its shoppers, who are overwhelmingly women. "Our customers are all about pop culture, celebrity, and dressing with individuality," says Payner. We already know that a shared experience is a powerful bonding tool. Women rewarded Bluefly with a 30 percent increase in new, unique visitors over the weeks in which the fourth-season promotion ran, and the week that winner Christian Siriano's collection launched on Bluefly, new, unique visitors rose 70 percent. Most important, sales rose 22 percent in the first quarter of 2008. Bluefly followed up its success by creating a promotion with the movie *Confessions of a Shopaholic* that was so integrated that the movie's official website was actually housed on Bluefly.com. "It's not enough to run one commercial on a few different shows," says Payner. "I'd rather be at every touchpoint of just one thing than all over the place."

It's not easy to reach women who are constantly on the move, but we know they do pay attention to their favorite TV shows and movies. The Bluefly/*Project Runway* campaign is a great example of speaking directly to women while they're already paying attention to something they enjoy, whether they've TiVo'd it or not.

Lessons for your business

Takeaways from Bluefly include:

- **Enthusiasm is contagious.**

  If your target audience is crazy about something, don't be afraid to join in and become an unabashed fan, too. It will help you connect with your female audience.

- **Find a way to give fans a piece of the action.**

  Even if it's just a close approximation, your customers may delight in getting something from you that they will always be able to associate with their favorite show, band, or movie. McDonald's has been doing this for years through its Happy Meal movie tie-ins, but the tactic is less common for adult women.

- **Unleash your nonpower players.**

  "Regular" employees of companies are perceived as more trustworthy than CEOs, especially since the economic collapse of 2008. Which means that perhaps it's time to unleash your unsung cube dwellers. Any one of your employees who is genuinely charming can be a face of your brand. Maybe not *the* face, but *a* face, particularly for the younger demographic. Bluefly featured a blog from its merchandising coordinator in addition to its CEO. In a world of reality TV, the person in the cubicle is often perceived as more interesting, and more credible, than the person in the corner office.

- **Go deep.**

In a fragmented media envirinment, it can be more powerful to go big with one property—if it's the right one—rather than spreading yourself thin.

Principles of Gender Appeal

MASTERCARD, method, and Bluefly effectively tap into the values of women's culture. To increase your own company's gender appeal, consider the following female fundamentals.

Improving the world around them

Generally speaking, women are drawn to products and services that make them feel like they're making the world better in some small way. Research shows that both cause marketing and "green" campaigns find their strongest audiences in women.[5] Women volunteer at higher rates than men do across all age groups and education levels.[6] Whole Foods Market, which bases its marketing on the premise "Feel Good About Where You Shop," is a textbook study in this concept. The company actively communicates with customers about its products and practices, and makes people feel as if their trip to the grocery store is, among other things, contributing to their health and that of their family members; helping to improve working conditions for organic farmers; and minimizing damage to the environment. Women who may not think twice about such things during the course of their normal routines can walk out of a Whole Foods feeling satisfied that they've done their bit for the world and for their own bodies, just by doing something as simple as buying organic meat and potatoes for dinner.

The ability to be organic, to be sustainable, and to improve the lives of workers in the world's poorest countries is a lot of bang for the buck from a quick trip to the grocery store. Most companies can't take social responsibility to the level of Whole Foods, but even small efforts—such as supporting local organizations in your own community—can have a big impact on women's perceptions of your brand. And take some cues from Whole Foods, such as educating customers about where your products come from and who makes them; those are applicable to companies of every size.

Finding beauty in the imperfect

Because women think people are fascinating, they're drawn to images and descriptions of people in marketing materials. People who are quirky and honest and who don't pretend to be perfect find a welcoming audience with women, as evidenced by the popularity of Oprah Winfrey, Ellen DeGeneres, and the success of the Dove "Campaign for Real Beauty," which features ordinary women instead of professional models.

Comedian Tina Fey and her ads for American Express are a great example of this aspect of gender appeal. American

Express' long-running marketing campaign "My Life, My Card" gives people insight into the personal and seemingly honest/quirky aspects of celebrities' lives. One of the most charming ads features Fey sitting under her desk, in a messy office strewn with crumpled papers, while her baby daughter sits in Fey's seat, typing on her computer. Fey and the product she's promoting seem accessible, appealing, and even endearing. People think, *I want to be her. She's talented, smart, happy, and successful, and she's not perfect, just like me. I'll have what she's having.*

Being a shrewd shopper

Being a shrewd shopper is a point of pride for most women, which means that it's important to articulate why your product or service is a great value. Ideally, this exercise can be done with style, because for women, value doesn't necessarily mean the lowest price—it means that whatever they've bought is worth more than they've paid for it.

Everybody's favorite cheap-chic destination, Target, consistently makes women feel smart about shopping at its stores, and the beauty of the brand is that its marketing is in sync with the actual customer experience. A winner of countless marketing awards, Target's team has a gift for showing mundane items such as vacuum cleaners in the hippest of graphic settings, and its design partnerships with people ranging from Michael Graves to Isaac Mizrahi add sizzle to the company's overall brand image.

Nothing from Target feels dumbed down. When it chooses designer partnerships with trendy up-and-comers instead of predictable household names, the chain not only saves money, it positions itself as in the know, while trusting its customers to recognize the talent of the designers, if not the names. This, in turn, makes its customers feel like Target has brought them in on something special that the big department stores haven't discovered yet. The company's motto, "Design for All," communicates that even people who like low prices deserve good design. Though many of the products Target sells are identical to those in the aisles of Wal-Mart and Kmart, its marketing has positioned the Minneapolis-based retailer as indisputably "downtown" instead of downmarket. Demonstrating that it's a true marketing decathlete, Target also promotes the fact that 5 percent of the company's income goes back to the local communities it serves, to the tune of $3 million per week.

Caring about others

Women are the primary caregivers for the world's children and elderly in every society in the world. According to Dr. Marianne Legato, the founder of Columbia University's Partnership for Gender-Specific Medicine, women's interest in caring for others is hypertrophied—or overly developed. There are many theories as to why. One of them is that the activities associated with having a child—pregnancy, birth, and breastfeeding—cause oxytocin levels to skyrocket in women.[7] Oxytocin is one of the bonding hormones that drive maternal behaviors, and its presence means that women may derive more genuine pleasure from caring for others than many men do.

Kleenex is running a wonderful marketing campaign, called "Let It Out," in which it encourages people to listen to each other, let out their emotions (into a nice, soft Kleenex), and not be ashamed of them. On its website, Kleenex has invited people to show they care for others by figuratively "giving" a Kleenex tissue (a tissue box icon) to anyone who might need one. People can post their emotional, personal stories on the company's website, and readers can "pass a Kleenex" to whomever they sympathize with most. It's a campaign with great gender appeal, executed with a light touch and tone. Kleenex has a history of creating marketing campaigns that resonate with women's caring nature, including the famous "Kleenex Says Bless You" campaigns from the 1980s.

What it does is more important than how it works

"What is this product going to do for me?" is the question every marketer should be able to answer, with brevity. Women are interested in practical descriptions, such as "This camera takes perfect shots that you can store easily, upload to your computer instantly, and share with your friends and family." Men tend to be more interested in the how, such as "This high-performance camera has optical image stabilization, 8 megapixels, and a 38-to-114-mm-equivalent f/2.8-to-4.9 3x optical zoom lens."

This insight mirrors the reality of men's and women's conversations. Women don't talk to each other about the technical specs of their purchases, but men do. It's not that women aren't *ever* interested in the technical details; it's just that they consider them far less interesting than the practical attributes. When it comes to women, it's important for your brand to have a good elevator pitch.

Women respond to messages about improving; men respond to messages about winning

Women consider themselves a work in progress. They're often engaged in an ongoing quest to improve themselves, their health, their surroundings, and the lives of their families.

Marketing messages that acknowledge that women's sense of achievement is something internal, and often tied to reaching their personal best, however they define it, are a great way to create gender appeal. Gold's Gym is running a campaign that breaks the mold of the health club industry's decades-long propensity to create campaigns that feature nothing but perfect bodies in spandex. The Gold's campaign is based on the theme "Know Your Own Strength," and it carries the message that strength is more than just a perfect body—it's both internal and external. One campaign shows a close-up of a woman's legs climbing on a StairMaster as words appear on the staircase, one after the other:

1st floor
2nd floor
12th floor
Penthouse
Empire State
Kilimanjaro
Everest
Olympus
The corporate ladder

The ad finishes with "Know your own strength."

This ad and others in the Gold's campaign communicate the message that a perfect body isn't the only goal of working out—it's also to feel strong physically and emotionally, so that you can meet the daily challenges of your life. It's a positive and unexpected message from a health club company that has a history of catering to the barbell set, and it has high gender appeal for women.

Women respond to personal stories and examples; men respond to factual information

Women's conversations are full of stories about the people in their lives. When men speak to each other, they tend to talk about things such as business, sports, world events, gadgets, politics, and cars. This is because if a man gets too personal, he may inadvertently expose a weakness or vulnerability. Socially speaking, it's more acceptable for men to deal in facts than in feelings. The reverse is true for women.

As in MasterCard's "Priceless" campaign, details about *people* are what make a conversation interesting to women. That's why they buy all those celebrity magazines with photo spreads that exclaim, "Look at Jennifer Aniston pumping gas . . . she's just like us!" For men, however, details about *things* are what make something interesting. Heated conversations about sports team statistics are just one example. Naturally, this has implications for marketing.

It's easy to notice the differences in your personal life. A few weeks ago, I was sitting in an airplane next to my husband, Erik, in the middle of a flight to New York. He was reading a magazine, and without looking up from it, he casually dropped a bomb. He told me his boss, Daniel, had gotten engaged the previous weekend.

This was huge news. We'd all been wondering when Daniel would pop the question to his girlfriend. My first thought was, *Erik waited to tell me this news flash until we were in midflight? It took us an hour to get to the airport in traffic, and he didn't think to mention it during all that time?*

I put down what I was reading and in a burst of enthusiasm looked straight at him and asked, "Well, what did he say?"

In a deadpan voice, and still looking at his magazine, Erik replied, "He said they got engaged." Pause. "What more is there to say?"

Was he kidding? There was plenty more to say. He was going to have to give me more information than this. I wanted to know where it happened, how Daniel did it, what he said, what she said, and if either of them cried. Astonishingly, Erik had no information about any of this. Nothing. Nada. Zip. I accused him of withholding information from me, but he said that it never occurred to him ask any of these questions. After a moment of frustrating silence (my frustration, not his), we just stared at each other in mutual incomprehension. Here's why: *Men talk to communicate information. Women talk to connect.*[8]

Remember when all those "up close and personal" segments started running during the Olympics? They were originally created by the ABC network to generate American interest in foreign athletes. It turns out that not only did these vignettes work, they were extremely attractive to women viewers, who were as interested in the backstage human dramas of the athletes as in the contests themselves. Women wanted to know who these people were and what motivated them to get up at the crack of dawn every morning for twenty years just to practice. They wanted the emotional connection to the athlete. For women, it's the people side of life that's the most interesting.

The next time you're at the beginning stages of creating a marketing strategy designed to appeal to women, consider this checklist of tactical marketing techniques that have proven female appeal:

- ✔ Storytelling
- ✔ Personal testimonials
- ✔ Before-and-after comparisons
- ✔ Tie-ins with worthy causes
- ✔ Humor (without victims, because women identify with victims in jokes)
- ✔ Compliments
- ✔ Self-deprecation
- ✔ Milestone references (anniversaries, birthdays, holidays)
- ✔ Life stage references (instead of age references)
- ✔ Woman as hero instead of product as hero
- ✔ Value messaging that makes women feel smart but not cheap
- ✔ Reassurance and justification for luxury products— guilt removal
- ✔ What something *does*—not how it works

Consider the Source: Public Relations

SUSIE, a mother of three in the San Francisco Bay Area, wasn't sure what to do about all the plastic water bottles in her home. She'd heard stories in the news recently about chemicals leaching from certain brands of bottles that posed a potential health hazard. She and her kids have an active lifestyle, and water bottles are always with them. She needed a trusted opinion on which kind to buy. So she turned to her local parenting group, the Marin Parents of Multiples, where she learned about a Swiss brand called Sigg that was 100 percent aluminum and leachproof. She immediately went out and bought four bottles, one for each member of her family. Her trusted source—a local parenting website and its community forum—had come through for her again.

The way Susie discovered Sigg is increasingly common. With so little time left over from work and family responsibilities, a busy mom like Susie can't and won't easily absorb marketing messages. She uses shortcuts to discover what she needs to know. Women are seekers of help, and they'll zero in on their most credible sources for advice, from girlfriends, mothers, and pediatricians to their favorite magazines, websites, blogs, and TV shows. Women's propensity to ask people for product advice comes both from a lack of time and from the importance placed on third-party credibility.

Women constantly have their antennae out for tips and advice and are happy when someone they trust has done the product research for them, whether it's a neighbor with a recommendation for a contractor, a magazine editor with a top-ten list, or a friend on Facebook who's just become a fan of a cool new band.

Third-party credibility is powerful with women. The reasons stem not only from living in an oversaturated marketing environment but also from childhood, where young girls learn that bragging is frowned upon in female culture. Girls learn fast that it's better to have someone else do their bragging for them. This applies to products as well as people:

women would rather have someone else tell them how great your product is, not necessarily you—hence the enduring popularity of *Consumer Reports* and the more recent successes of websites such as TripAdvisor.com and Yelp.com, and recommendations from sites like Amazon, iTunes, and CNET. According to the Edelman Trust Barometer, an annual global study of consumer influence from one of the world's largest public relations agencies, one of the most credible sources of information about a company is a "person like yourself." The least credible source cited in the study was corporate or product advertising.

When you combine this information about trust with two other aspects of female culture—that product knowledge is a form of social currency, and that women feel compelled to tell their friends about new finds—then it's easy to see why women place so much value on credible opinions.

All of which leads to public relations as one of the most effective ways for women to learn about your product or service. The power of PR comes from the third-party credibility of having *other* people say great things about you, which makes it an excellent marketing vehicle for reaching and influencing women. Just the mention of your brand in an environment that your customers consider credible can have an impact. This is why everyone in the world wants to promote a book on *The Oprah Winfrey Show,* give away a product on *The Ellen Degeneres Show,* or get featured as an editor's pick in a magazine.

The problem is that while many companies dream of getting third-party endorsements from experts and influential people, they aren't prepared to commit the resources needed to get them. While "free" publicity seems free, it rarely is, since there are significant, hard costs in terms of the labor and proactivity it takes to get your product or service in the hands of the journalists, bloggers, celebrities, and producers who sway opinion. The perception that publicity is free is a false one, yet it persists.

The other reason it's difficult for some people to rationalize public relations spending is because there are no guarantees. You can send a product to one of Oprah's producers, for example, but you will never know if Oprah herself will ever do anything with it, or even see it, unless you've developed a relationship with that producer. The same is true with most public relations efforts. Putting energy and resources behind proactive relationship-building with the media and people who influence your target audience can pay off substantially—especially when it comes to working with bloggers, who many women feel are the very definition of "a person like yourself."

Spreading the Message Through Women Bloggers

THE courting of women bloggers is a public relations strategy that has exploded in importance in recent years. There are about thirty-six million reasons why. This is the number of women who participate in the blogosphere weekly: there are about fifteen million women who write blogs, and twenty-one million who read and/or post to blogs on a weekly basis.[9]

That's a lot of women. People always ask me, Who are they? What are they writing about? And who reads them? The majority of women bloggers are between the ages of twenty-nine and forty-four, and a significant percentage of them are in the life stage of early motherhood. These so-called mommy bloggers write about their lives and the juggling act of managing households full of babies and young kids. They seek community with other mothers who are doing the same.

"Blogs are the new back fence," says BlogHer cofounder Jory Des Jardins, who runs a network of more than twenty-seven hundred women's blogs in a business based near San Francisco. Take a drive through a suburban neighborhood in the middle of a weekday and you'll see what she means: in many places, you'll find silence and empty streets. With most women working outside the home, those who choose to stay home and raise their kids can feel isolated and alone. Blogging is a way for them to meet their "neighbors"—whether it's a few streets or a few states over. Women who work outside the home can feel isolated, too, and may be uncomfortable sharing their parenting issues at work. These women use blogs as sounding boards for stories and advice along the journey of motherhood.

Because bloggers write about their own lives, their opinions are perceived as authentic—and therefore credible—and carry weight with readers. They write about the everyday aspects of their lives, such as going to visit their kids at school, trying a new brand of diapers, or shopping at their favorite online stores. Often, they talk about their feelings and the challenges of getting through the day with their sanity intact. Since moms are such a powerful spending force, marketers are wooing the mommy bloggers accordingly.

Enter networks such as BlogHer, which serve as a clearinghouse for companies looking to place their ads on women's blogs on a mass scale. BlogHer sells space on its members' blogs in the same way other media sell space— on a cost-per-thousand basis. Every blogger who allows an ad to be placed "above the fold" on her blog receives a small stipend. It has become a media vehicle that agencies buy in virtually the same way that traditional advertising is purchased.

From a public relations standpoint, many companies' strategies with bloggers run deep. More and more companies are developing full-blown blogger relations programs. Major players such as Procter & Gamble and Disney have invited mommy bloggers to meet with executives, discuss products, tour their facilities, and provide feedback, in hopes that the bloggers will walk away with a positive experience of the brand. "Field trips" to company headquarters are becoming quite common. Most of the companies that fund these all-expenses-paid blogger trips don't require the bloggers to write about their experiences—that approach would likely backfire—but the presumption is that they will write positive stories, and most do. The bloggers will often show pictures from these corporate events; they'll discuss their interviews with executives; they'll Twitter directly from the event as it's happening; and many will rave about being treated like queens. For women who are out of the workforce, an all-expense-paid trip is often a welcome break, and a chance to feel valued by high-profile corporate executives. In return, the companies get a grass-roots audience exposed to their brand in an authentic and credible way.

For companies in the business-to-business space, industry bloggers can be hugely influential, particularly when it comes to technology. Adam Schokora, a Shanghai-based social media strategist who studies bloggers for Edelman Digital, gives some practical advice on how to reach the world of industry bloggers. "It's not how many people you're talking to online, it's who," he says. "Ten people might influence hundreds of thousands of people, so focusing on those ten is the smartest strategy." In the United States, one way to determine the most highly trafficked bloggers is through ranking services such as Alexa and Technorati, which compile lists of the most widely visited sites.

The best way to approach bloggers is to read their entries over a significant period of time so that when you approach them, you can tailor your pitch to what interests them—and their readership—most. It's the same way that most companies approach journalists: knowing their beat, their past stories, and their topics of interest. One company, baby products manufacturer Graco, started its own blog in which parents on the Graco corporate staff write about their experiences with parenthood. The Graco corporate blog links to dozens of other mommy blogs, and the company hosts blogger get-togethers across the country so that these scribes can meet each other in person.

What will be interesting to watch over the next five years is whether bloggers' credibility diminishes as they begin to accept more advertising, product placements, and corporate largesse. It would be ironic if the very people who seek bloggers' endorsements because of their credibility—marketers—end up undermining it through their efforts. Indeed, this very issue has led the Federal Trade Commission to establish guidelines mandating that bloggers disclose "freebies" and compensation for the products and brands they promote.

Women: The Original Social Network

It used to be that marketers wanted people to love their products; now they will happily settle for "like"—at least on Facebook, the largest social networking site in the world. Leveraging the viral power of social networks such as Facebook, Twitter, Yelp, LinkedIn, MySpace, and Flickr, as well as the vast number of online community groups, has become an all-consuming quest for consumer businesses. And it's no wonder. Social networks are like big rooms where millions of people are gathered, talking enthusiastically. Marketers, of course, want to get in on the conversation, but this is easier said than done. Typically, the goal is to recruit as many fans and friends as possible for products and campaigns. It's interesting to consider that for nearly the entire span of human history, being a friend has meant that at the very least, one had to be human. What kind of "friendship" can a person realistically forge with an inanimate object, like a brand of mustard? Marketers are working day and night to push the boundaries and find out.

As with bloggers, but on a much larger scale, the mass documentation of people's lives makes it inevitable that they will mention the brands, products, movies, restaurants, and service providers with which they interact.

Getting involved in people's conversations without being viewed as intrusive, slick, or overtly promotional is challenging. One can imagine the agony of producing an expensive YouTube commercial that goes nowhere, while an amateur's 30-second shot of his cat sneezing becomes a global hit. The truth is that like any other form of media, consumers aren't in it for the advertising. And while social networks have become sophisticated at segmenting consumers' profiles for the benefit of advertisers, a great way to get talked about online is to first identify which sex is doing most of the talking. Can you guess?

Globally, women spend more time on social networking sites than men do.[10] This isn't surprising, given the fact that women have long driven social communication in the offline world. Females constitute the majority of Facebook users (57 percent) and are more active on the site than men. They have 8 percent more friends and supply the majority (62 percent) of sharing and updating.[11] As we have already learned, women routinely recommend products to friends and ask for opinions from other people. When they find a great product, women feel it's their *obligation* to tell their friends. Enter social networks, which magnify these natural female behaviors and make women's "word-of-mouth" publicity even more invaluable to businesses. Facebook COO Sheryl Sandberg put it this way: *"The world's gone social. And women are more social than men."*[12]

As people share their lives through status updates, tweeting, posting photos, and voicing their opinions, they are often "advertising" products on social networks in the most credible way possible without necessarily realizing it. Every time someone poses a question like *"Any ideas for what I should get my husband for Valentine's Day?"* the word-of-mouth recommendations start flying. Naturally, the vast majority of women who answer such questions don't see themselves as promoting a product; they're simply having a conversation with a friend and trying to be helpful.

The principles of gender appeal are important to keep in

mind when it comes to reaching women on social networks. The following are three ways to incorporate gender appeal into your social networking strategies:

- **Help your customers look like heroes in the eyes of their friends.**

  Supporting a worthy cause, for example, is almost always a great idea for humanitarian reasons, and it offers the added benefit of making supporters feel proud about helping the world become a better place in some small way. Recently, I pressed the "like" button on Facebook for Kenmore home appliances, and as a result of my click, Kenmore sent a dozen cookies to U.S. soldiers overseas. My small act of kindness (which was actually Kenmore's act of kindness) was displayed on my status update, making both me—and Kenmore—look like heroes.

- **Engage women in conversations around a topic or issue that you'd like to be associated with.**

  In most categories, it's unrealistic to expect people to carry on lengthy conversations about a specific product or brand. Try engaging women in discussions *related* to your product category, not just the product itself. The idea is to engage women in conversations with which you'd like your brand to be *associated*. For example, a paper towel brand might initiate discussions about how to keep a healthy and green home, and ask consumers to share their ideas. Don't just offer free product in exchange for publicity; it's considered gauche. "The days of 'mention my product and I'll give you a free one' are over," says Megan Calhoun, founder of the influential social networking group SocialMoms.

- **Incorporate a photographic element whenever you can.**

Women are the photo sharers, memory keepers, and documenters of family events. They are more involved in photo-sharing sites than men are,[13] and are often on the hunt for good photos to post online. Challenge yourself to get your customers involved with your brand through photography. The possibilities are endless—a pet store could easily have a "me and my pet" photo contest on Facebook where the person with the most "likes" for their photo gets a year's worth of free dog food. Travel destinations could run a contest for the best family vacation photo, with a great prize that drives consumers to tell their friends "Vote for my picture!" Brands with mascots could create applications that allow consumers to create images that feature their own face next to the mascot's. When it comes to your customers, photography is a great way to create an interactive experience and get included in their conversations in a dynamic, natural, and viral way.

What to Do When Your Product Is a "Me Too"

MANY people have the job of selling products that are comparable to (meaning no better or worse than) those of the competition, hence the need for good marketing. Innovative products are few and far between. So what happens when you really struggle to come up with a compelling reason for women to buy your product instead of someone else's?

Or worse, what happens when you realize there really is no compelling reason for them to buy it instead of someone else's?

It's not uncommon. Most products in most categories are pretty good, or they wouldn't survive. In my view, there's only one solution to this problem: *provide better customer service than anyone else.*

We're talking about customer service in a chapter on marketing because in real life, customer service and marketing are the same thing. The only place customer service and marketing aren't one and the same is in the halls of corporations. All too often, they're housed in separate silos, which means the people in these departments don't interact or work with each other on a regular basis.

From billboards to TV commercials to online ads and YouTube videos, most marketing energy goes into a full frontal assault on the senses. But what happens *after* the customer is acquired is just as important, if not more so. It's an enormous opportunity for brand differentiation with women. That's because great customer service is still rare. Research shows that 61 percent of people feel that "most of the time, the service people I deal with don't care much about me or my needs."[14] Some industries are worse than others. "When I'm having a problem with my cable company, I have to work myself up all day to get the strength to call them," says forty-five-year-old Theresa. "I know I need to set aside an hour, minimum, and that I will be angry and depressed afterwards. Just knowing I have to talk to them ruins my whole day."

We're all exposed to an endless parade of marketing messages, which means that expectations are high when we make a buying decision. Yet it seems that service after the sale is too often forgotten in the thrill of the hunt for customers. Once the customer is snagged, the wooing is over and the romance is dead. There is no shortage of terrible customer service stories and rants on the Web about every industry. You probably have several of your own. To be confronted by bad service after aggressive wooing puts many people in an adversarial relationship with the very companies that are supposed to be serving them.

With so many options, people are less willing to put up with bad service. The fact that customer service is a consumer hot button also makes it a major opportunity for differentiation. We're going to devote the rest of the chapter to discussing how it can be implemented most effectively, since most of your competitors are probably doing a lousy job of it.

Gender matters here as well

The research firm Yankelovich recently commissioned a study about customer service in which it asked people whether it had improved over the previous five years. The results showed a gender gap: 44 percent of women felt that service had gotten worse, compared to just 33 percent of men.[15] For several reasons, women have a low tolerance for poor customer service. One is that they interact so frequently with customer service people, given their role as chief purchaser for their households. Unsurprisingly, these interactions can be less-than-joyful experiences.

The second reason women resent poor service is because it wastes their time. Encountering long hold times or inefficient automated menus on the phone is stressful. Finally (and this is the reason that's not so obvious), women have a distinct point of view about how people should be treated, based on female culture and the unique qualities of the female brain.

Mothers teach kids about fairness from the moment a toddler starts interacting with other children. They drill their children with instructions about sharing with their siblings and friends and tell them thousands of times to say please and thank you. Mothers everywhere have antennae for small injustices, because it's their job to notice when these happen with their children. As young girls, women were taught to be sweet, polite, and modest, and that's still how little girls are socialized, right alongside all those "girl power" messages. Women are expected to be caring, fair, and the champion of the underdog. There's a reason Miss Manners isn't Mr. Manners. There's a reason Dear Abby isn't Dear Frank. So when a woman is on the receiving end of a bad customer service experience . . . well, as they say, hell hath no fury like it.

The psychiatrist and brain researcher Dr. Daniel Amen agrees. "Women have an expectation of how things should be," he says. "If they don't believe they're being treated fairly, they get angry. And when they get angry, it's like a loop that runs over and over in the brain. They will stew about it longer than men will. That's the front part of their brain working hard—the worry part."

Automate this

Obviously, corporate bean counters think they are doing the right thing by using cheaper, twenty-four-hour call centers in India and elsewhere, and by automating customer service or using voice recognition systems. Yet they may not fully understand the problems this can pose for customer satisfaction. While there's certainly nothing wrong with automation, it's how it's used that's an issue. There are dozens of routine transactions for which people are thrilled to have a self-service option. How many people could survive without cash machines? But people appreciate automation only when it makes their lives better, not worse.

Customer service call centers are the white-hot nucleus of consumer anger. Being forced to pick from only five categories on a menu of reasons for a call, all of which may be irrelevant, is infuriating to the person angrily pressing buttons on the other end of the line. Even worse is being charged or penalized for talking to an actual human being. Research shows that the majority of people still want to talk to a real person in a wide variety of customer service situations, including when they're getting a diagnostic health test, seeking technical support, buying or selling stocks, checking out at grocery stores, checking in for a flight, and depositing money into a bank account, among many other transactions.[16] Because there are vast differences in people's technical prowess, providing both high-quality automated and human options is the ideal.

There are numerous implications for gender differences in customer service. The fact that women use more words than men and are most interested in the details of any conversation is just one aspect that could be reflected in training for customer call resolution and scripting. The fact that many women run their errands during the lunch hour is another implication for the timing of customer service staffing schedules.

Companies should consider taking a fresh look at customer service measurements and standards, especially as they relate to marketing. We all know that the two departments must work in sync for maximum effectiveness, but the ugly truth is that most of the time they don't. High awareness on the front end of marketing is considerably less meaningful if consumer loyalty is decreased on the back end. The Internet has increased expectations and, frankly, made it more dangerous to provide bad service, because of the propensity of people to rant about it publicly. As one manager of a four-star hotel told me, "Websites like Tripadvisor.com are the bane of my existence."

It's not what you say, it's how you say it

The age-old irony is that the people entrusted to deliver the brand in its most intimate form—through one-on-one communication in customer call centers—are usually the lowest paid and least respected in a corporation. They don't live in the same neighborhoods as middle management, and you can bet they don't go to the same parties. Hiring better-educated people is going to become increasingly important as e-mail becomes a more popular vehicle for customer service, making good grammar skills necessary.

The elephant in the room is the reality of offshoring customer service. Opinion Research Corporation, a market research firm, conducts a regular series of studies on "ouch points" that impact customer service. What was the number one "ouch point" in a recent study? Representatives who are hard to understand because of a thick accent. This data is underscored by the Yankelovich study, which shows that 48 percent of people are outraged by the fact that companies try to keep the prices of their products down by moving customer-service call centers overseas.

With or without the language barrier, offshoring can generate ill will because it says to your customers, *We are trying to deal with you as cheaply as possible, no matter how much money you have spent with us.* It can feel like a slap in the face when the companies that spend so much time chasing us, interrupting our days with nonstop marketing messages in elevators, buses, and even toilet stalls, would actually prefer not to speak to us when we try to initiate contact, or would attempt to do so in the cheapest way possible.

Southwest Airlines: Customer Service with LUV

Isn't it ironic that the most profitable airline in the industry also has the best customer service?

Since 1987, Southwest Airlines has consistently received the fewest overall customer complaints of any U.S. airline.[17] When someone calls Southwest Airlines' customer service line, the phone rolls right over to a real human being. The company doesn't outsource its customer service department, and its people are empowered to deal with complex issues right over the phone. Strangely enough for corporate

America, the customer service representatives are not only nice, they're funny. It's disarming.

I suppose when you have a founder (Herb Kelleher) who doesn't hesitate to dress in drag or settle lawsuits with arm wrestling, the culture trickles down to customer service. "We hire on personality," says Jim Ruppel, the understated guy who runs the customer relations department for Southwest. "We train our employees to use common sense and good judgment, and ask them to have fun—and to encourage our customers to have fun, too." If you've ever flown Southwest, you're aware the same philosophy is clearly encouraged with their flight attendants, who are known to sing during announcements and tell salty jokes as they hand out the nuts. The airline also has the best profitability record, on-time record, and safety record in the industry. Southwest staffs its call centers with employees who've been indoctrinated in the company's empowering-yet-laid-back culture. "We don't offshore customer service because we have the philosophy that no one will treat our customers as well as Southwest's own employees will," says Ruppel.

And treat them well they do. Southwest doesn't suffer from the traditionally high turnover rates of most customer service centers. Ruppel credits this to the fact that employees are given latitude to use their own good judgment in resolving customer issues. "Essentially, they have the same authority I do," he says. "We have a quality assurance process, but we give them the opportunity to formulate what they think is the best customer response, and this is what keeps their job satisfaction a little bit higher," he explains. "When I lose people, I usually lose them to other departments at Southwest, who love hiring these people because they are willing to make decisions."

I interviewed Melissa, a customer of Southwest Airlines who is a mother of two and a native of St. Louis. Southwest showed her exemplary customer service on what turned out to be the worst day of her life. This is her story.

I fly Southwest all the time with my two young daughters, because my husband is in a medical residency program, so it's either fly by myself with the kids to see the grandparents or don't fly at all.

When my daughter Megan was a young toddler, I was flying to St. Louis on Southwest when she had a seizure on the airplane. She had never had one before, and was shaking uncontrollably, completely unresponsive. I was a terrified new mother traveling alone. We were about thirty minutes from St. Louis, flying over cornfields, and there was no place to land the plane. We had to wait to get to the St. Louis airport. The Southwest flight attendant was incredible to me. He kept telling me, "She's breathing, she's going to be okay," and helped calm me down. He called 911 to order paramedics to meet us at the gate, and he had my parents paged inside the airport. He held my child a lot and kept informing me of what was going on. He never left my side.

Sure enough, when we landed, everyone let me off the plane first, and there were paramedics standing at the gate ready for me. They took one look at my daughter and knew instantly that she'd had a febrile seizure, caused by a quick spike in temperature, and that there would be no residual damage. My story has a happy ending, but it doesn't end there. It wasn't just the individual

Southwest flight attendant that was so special, it was the company itself.

Before we had taken off that day, my daughter had made friends with another little girl she met at the gate. During Megan's seizure on the plane, I could see this young girl watching the whole episode from a nearby row. Her eyes were like saucers, and I knew she was terrified that her new little friend was going to die. I wrote Southwest after the incident to praise them for their service, and to let them know that Megan was fine. I also mentioned my concern for the other little girl, who I was afraid would be too terrified to ever step on an airplane again. I knew the little girl's first name, but I didn't know her last name, and I was hoping Southwest could find her and let her know that her little friend had made it.

Soon afterward, Southwest wrote to let me know that they had indeed identified the little girl and written to her family on my behalf. They gave me a copy of the letter they had sent to the family. Southwest also sent me a personalized letter saying they were happy to hear that Megan was all right, along with a gift of a stuffed toy airplane for her. The company and its people were amazing on what was, without a doubt, the worst day of my life, and their customer service afterward was just as incredible. As long as I have a choice, I will always fly Southwest, and I have told this story about their wonderful service to more people than I can remember.

Southwest Airlines' customer service mirrors its marketing as well as its corporate culture. With a profitability record unmatched by any other airline, the folks at Southwest have demonstrated that when you take care of your customers, the business takes care of itself.

Lessons for your business

Takeaways from Southwest Airlines include:

- **Customer service policies are a reflection of your brand.**
If what you do in customer service isn't reinforcing your brand, it's probably hurting it, as well as decreasing the effectiveness of your marketing budget.

- **To consumers, customer service is just another aspect of marketing.**
The personality people see in commercials and advertisements is what they expect when they contact your company. Take the time to call or e-mail your company yourself, to see whether there's a disconnect between your marketing and your customer service messaging.

- **Great customer service drives word-of-mouth publicity.**
When women have an exceptional personal experience with a brand, they are apt to tell everyone they know. In a highly commoditized world, it can be a powerful differentiator for your business.

Customer Service Is Marketing

As this chapter comes to a close, it bears repeating: *customer service is marketing,* especially to your women customers. The next time you gather your team together to strategize about marketing plans, consider the back end of the process, not just the front end. All the things that happen *after* you acquire your customer are part of the marketing process, too.

Checklist for Customer Service with Female Gender Appeal

✔ Offer as many different customer-service contact methods as possible

✔ Find out the gender split of your customer service inquiries, and determine if existing training methods and procedures adequately accommodate gender differences in communication styles.

✔ Prominently display your customer service number on your website.

✔ Allow people to hit zero to get to an agent immediately, anytime during the call.

✔ Don't assume an automated menu of five possible questions fits every caller. Broaden the menu items to include a category for "other."

✔ Allow customers to recontact a specific representative, so they don't have to start over every time they contact your company about an unresolved issue.

✔ Allow outbound calling from the call center, so that representatives can call back customers with answers to their questions.

✔ Consider welcoming customers with a greeting from your CEO, thanking people for their business.

✔ Identify your best customers and create a customer-care service line and program especially for them.

✔ Make call center training and scripting more flexible, to allow representatives to ask and respond to open-ended questions, and to make judgment calls without putting the caller on hold to check with a supervisor.

✔ Don't charge people for making a transaction through a human being. Last time I checked, we are all still human.

6

THE LAST
THREE FEET

Fundamentals of Selling to Women

No matter how many times a woman sees an ad, or how much research she's conducted online, the critical purchasing moment often comes down to that "last three feet of the sale." This is when she's standing in front of a product or talking directly to a salesperson with her hands on her hips, trying to decide whether to buy. At this juncture, all bets are off. It's here, in this moment, that mistakes are frequently made and sales are lost—simply because women have different expectations of the sales process than men do.

Understanding these differences can have a major impact on your closing rates. As a bonus, it's a skill your competitors probably haven't mastered. Freudian jokes aside, learning what women want—from a salesperson, at least—is a straightforward exercise based on understanding female culture. Whatever you're selling, the sex of the person you're selling it to makes an enormous difference in how your pitch is received. Even if you aren't formally in sales, everyone is selling something. And no amount of automation can replace the fundamentals of good selling techniques.

In business, selling usually occurs in one of three ways: face-to-face situations, brick-and-mortar retail establishments, and the online environment. This chapter tackles all three, starting with the most traditional sales technique of all: face-to-face selling.

There is no shortage of sales experts in this world, but most sales training programs don't address the issue of gender. Sales coaches and seminars overlook the simple question of whether the buyer is a man or a woman, and how that factor impacts the purchasing process. This is a huge oversight, because there is quite possibly nothing more significant. Sales is simply a form of communication, after all, and communication is where men's and women's styles differ most.

In my sales training seminars, I coach companies on how to increase sales by making women feel great about the experience. It all boils down to the following principles.

Principles of Face-to-Face Selling to Women

Women are evaluating the salesperson as much as the product

The first principle to remember is that women will try to determine if a sales representative is a "good person" before doing business with him or her. This is especially true when it comes to big-ticket purchases like cars, appliances, and home furnishings, as well as almost any kind of financial service. The higher the price, the more she has at stake, and consequently she wants to buy from someone she feels she can trust. During the consideration process, women will fast-forward to a worst-case scenario of something going wrong after the sale, and they'll try to imagine whether they could count on the salesperson if it does. All things being equal, women will buy from someone who they feel "deserves" their sale. They are often willing to pay more for better service and the peace of mind that comes from it. A bad sales experience can kill a woman's intention to buy, no matter how much she wants the product.

"I was in an appliance store once, and this salesperson started talking about himself as we were walking down the aisle to the refrigerator section," said Katie, a fifty-something Texan in need of a new fridge. "He asked me about my business, and I told him I was in real estate. I could tell he was just trying to make conversation, but he started rambling about how he used to be in real estate and didn't make any money at it, and now he was working in this particular store, where making money was 'like shooting fish in a barrel.' All I could think of was, 'Does he really think he's impressing me by talking this way?'

"He didn't ask me any questions about what I wanted, and just started opening a bunch of refrigerator doors and talking about the products and the prices. A few minutes later his name was called over the loudspeaker, and he went to take a phone call. I seized the opportunity and practically ran out the front door, saying to one of his colleagues, 'Tell him that this fish is leaving.' The sad part was that I really needed a refrigerator and would have preferred to buy one at that store, since I had already driven there, but there was no way I was going to give that guy my business. I haven't been back to the store since, and that was two years ago."

Katie's story illustrates that since women's and men's communications styles are different, what might work well in male culture—bravado and assertive displays of competence—can be off-putting for women. It's incumbent upon salespeople to learn the cultural norms of female conversational styles, or risk turning off their customers without ever understanding why.

Women factor in the needs of people who aren't there

When women shop, they constantly evaluate how their purchases might impact the people they care about most. They automatically factor in the needs and opinions of these friends, family members, and colleagues, even if they are the sole decision maker in a transaction. It's important to address these absent influencers during the sales process by asking your prospect if there are other people who will be using the product or involved with it in some way. By doing so, you may be able to surface unspoken barriers to sale. Think of these absent people as a woman's mental version of a Broadway cast. It's up to you to find out who else is in her play.

"When my husband and I bought a family car, we wanted an SUV, but we made sure to buy one with a handle inside the door so that my elderly mother could get in and out of it easily," said Jill, a thirty-something mother of three. "Some of the SUVs have a really high step-up. And even though my mom lives in Iowa and only visits three or four times a year, I still felt that it was important that she be able to get in and out of our car with no trouble, and that was a big factor in our purchasing decision." Jill's elderly mother didn't accompany her on her new-car search, and doesn't even live in her state, but she was there as an invisible part of Jill's decision-making process.

Women are more interested in product benefits than specs

As we learned in the last chapter, women are far more interested in the *what* than in the *why*. It's more powerful to say, "This side-by-side refrigerator/freezer can hold sixteen frozen pizzas," than to say, "This side-by-side refrigerator/freezer is thirty cubic feet." Cubic feet and other commonly used measurements that describe size just aren't meaningful to most people. The same thing goes for acronyms, the scourge of business-to-business selling experiences. Forget them. Instead, speak in practical terms and paint pictures with stories.

I once called Allstate to check on pricing for auto insurance, and instead of leaping right into a complicated discussion of premiums, deductibles, and liabilities, the salesperson painted pictures of how I would use the service, through stories like this: "Imagine if you got caught in a snowstorm on the side of the road on Thanksgiving Day and you had family coming over for dinner. If you got an Allstate plan, we'd make sure you got home quickly and safely." Wow. Painting such a vivid picture had a more powerful effect on me than any discussion of policy terms ever could. The policy discussions would come later, but capturing my imagination at the beginning of the sales process was the most important part.

Women are taught from childhood that talking about money is impolite

Attitudes about price negotiation are largely cultural. In many parts of the world, a woman's ability to negotiate is a point of pride, and bargaining is an enjoyable pastime for both buyer and seller. Not so in the West, where the bargaining economy is long gone (with the notable exception of eBay). Western women are taught from an early age that talking about money publicly is inappropriate, and this can make discussions about pricing uncomfortable for the female buyer. Whenever you can, be specific about why something is priced the way it is, and demonstrate good, better, and best options to give your prospect a choice. Most important, bring up the price yourself, before she has to ask.

Women appreciate having someone edit their options

In general, editing a customer's options is better than providing too many. She values her time, and therefore values your ability to save it. Depending on your product category, you can anticipate that a woman will be interested in knowing what option most people buy (it's human nature) or what you would buy if you were in her situation, so be sure to have those answers ready.

"I had a surprisingly great experience buying cell phones," said Amy, an executive who went to a Verizon store on a mission to buy phones for herself, her husband, and her eleven-year-old son. "I walked into the store and there were cell phones all over the wall, and my heart sank. I thought, *How am I going to decide between all of them? This is going to be a nightmare.*

"I was lucky enough to get a great salesperson who basically took me by the hand. First, I told her that I was clumsy and that I always drop my phones, so she gave me the two sturdiest phones in the store to pick from. Then I told her about my eleven-year-old son. She showed me a phone that would fit easily into his pants pocket—since that's where he'll end up carrying it—and that also had a good keyboard lock so that he wouldn't accidentally call China. Then my husband explained that he had never had a PDA (personal digital assistant) before, so she showed him the middle-of-the-road BlackBerry that was perfect for a first-timer. I had been dreading this shopping experience, but the salesperson made it pleasant by narrowing the options for us in a way that wasn't overwhelming." When it comes to selling to women, sometimes less is more.

When she says she'll think about it, she probably means it

It's shocking how many salespeople don't follow up with a potential female buyer once she has uttered the words "I need to think about it." Men often believe this comment is code for "I'm not interested." This is a mistake. Women put a lot of pressure on themselves to get a purchase right. They'll want to go home and talk about it with the people closest to them. They'll want to conduct more research on your product or company. They might want more time to consider the purchase away from you, without any pressure. Most likely, they will be impressed if you actually contact them to follow up. Women want to buy from someone who values their business. Following up after a sales call is one of the best and easiest ways to demonstrate that you do.

Women want to know their business is appreciated

It's important to demonstrate appreciation for women's business, whether it's through a personal thank-you note, a discount on a future purchase, a free giveaway, or some other thoughtful expression of gratitude. Women expect this kind of treatment when they spend their hard-earned money (or their company's hard-earned money) with you. Treat them right and they will spread the good word. I bought a Diane von Furstenberg dress in the fall, and eight months later received a birthday card from the company inviting me back with a $50 gift card "present." The gesture instantly endeared me to a brand of which I was already fond. And, yes, I went right back in and bought a dress. And now I'm telling you about it. See what happens when a woman has a great sales experience?

Selling Yourself to Female Customers: A Primer

SELLING a product is one thing; selling yourself is quite another. Selling to women successfully requires both. The most important thing to remember when selling to women is this: no matter what your product or service, you're really only selling one thing, and that's *help*. If what you're offering doesn't enhance her life, her work, or her family's life, then you're wasting her time and probably your own, too. So forget about the specifics of what you're selling, and reframe it in your mind as selling help.

The easiest path to "yes" from a female customer is through listening and asking open-ended questions. Rocket science it's not, but then again, good listening skills aren't common. When given the chance, women are likely to tell you everything you need to know to customize a pitch and make the sale. Suddenly the information that you might find trivial in any other context is liquid gold, as long as you can actually listen.

Take the story of Stacy, a woman in Dallas who went to buy a thank-you gift at the new Vera Bradley handbag store in her neighborhood.

I had never gone into a Vera Bradley store, but I needed a gift and heard that the store had some really beautiful things. I walked inside, and the place was decorated like someone's living room, which I loved. The store manager walked over to me, and I explained that I needed a thank-you gift. Instead of asking me for my price range, she asked why I was giving the gift. She wanted to hear what I was thanking the person for, so she could help me pick out just the right thing. I buy a lot of gifts, and no salesperson had ever asked me that question before.

I told her it was for someone I'd never met, who had returned to me an important file I'd left in the back of an airplane seat. The file was priceless—my father had just died, and I was the executor of his will, and it had all his important documents in it, including his checkbook, his bank account records, and his last will and testament.

The sales manager agreed that the woman who returned this to me deserved a pretty special gift.

She helped me pick out a great tote bag, then stuffed it with matching little freebies, and said, "This way when she opens it, she'll find one surprise after another." Then she told me that Vera Bradley had free gift wrapping and shipping, as well as a card I could send with the gift. Usually when I buy a gift, the job is only half done—I know it will take me another week to get around to shipping it. I walked out of the Vera Bradley store and I was done. I couldn't believe it. That was my first experience with this store and I will go back there again and again for gifts, because of that sales manager and the company's amazingly convenient shipping policy.

The sales manager at Vera Bradley made an effort to listen to *why* a product was being purchased, and in the process gave the kind of help that created a new fan for the brand. In addition to listening, there are a host of other techniques that can make all the difference between success and failure with women customers.

- **Make eye contact.**

If there is a woman waiting for you while you are dealing with someone else, nod and make eye contact to acknowledge her existence. She may quietly seethe if you don't.

- **Let her speak.**

Women are socialized to wait their turn to speak and not to interrupt. Taking turns talking is something ingrained in women from childhood, when they would take turns in role-playing games. Men, on the other hand, have a habit of interrupting each other to make their points, which is perfectly acceptable in male culture. Men's conversational style can be challenging and even provocative. Some men will take a devil's advocate position in a conversation just to keep things interesting. In a sales transaction with women, this style can be fatal.

Too often salespeople will talk nonstop to demonstrate their knowledge, and forget to give their female prospect a chance to say something. Like the man in the Texas appliance store, they will incorrectly assume that if a woman wanted to say something, she'd interrupt. Chances are she won't—she'll just leave, as Katie did, and he'll tell himself she was never a serious buyer to begin with.

When making your presentation or pitch, take a breath, and give the prospect a moment to say what's on her mind. Forcing yourself to stay silent for a few moments is a powerful tool. Everyone hates an awkward silent moment and will try to fill it; this is especially true with women. If you let the crickets chirp, you may end up hearing exactly what's on her mind, and then you can customize your pitch accordingly.

- **Explain without patronizing.**

Straddle the fine line between underexplaining and overexplaining by letting the customer be your guide. Prompt her by saying things like "Stop me if I'm telling you something you already know" or posing a simple question, such as "Would you like me to go into detail about any specific features of this service?" In all likelihood, she will ask you to home in on just the features she cares about most.

- **Repeat her statements.**

Women are sometimes reluctant to ask too many questions during the sales process because they don't want to appear uninformed and thus an easy target. Save her the trouble of asking you dozens of questions by letting her talk and then repeating her statements back to her as questions: "What I'm hearing you say is that you'd like to find a midrange option. Is that right?" When you get a positive response, it gives you license to go into detail on that particular aspect of the product or service. This technique also demonstrates that you've been listening to her, which women usually find impressive.

- **Identify her biggest concern.**

It may be because she doesn't want to insult you or hurt your feelings, but women are often hesitant to bring up their greatest concern about what you're selling. If you ask her directly, she's more likely to tell you what's on her mind. I once went to a sales presentation in which I was asked, "What is the one thing that concerns you most about choosing us as your vendor?" I was stunned by the blunt question, and it compelled me to say that I was concerned that the senior-level people in the room wouldn't be the people I'd be working with on a day-to-day basis. The vendor had the opportunity to convince me that it wasn't true, and so I hired them.

- **You are a reflection of your brand.**

Women will notice everything about your selling environment, from how messy your desk is to the stain on your shirt. For most women, cleanliness equals competence, and also respect—for yourself, for your customers, and for your business.

- **Be nice to others.**

Women pay attention to how you treat coworkers and servicepeople. They also evaluate your company's reputation. This comes into play in a big way in business-to-business sales. The rule applies all the way from big things (your company's support of social causes) to small things (how you speak to your underlings). If you take a female prospect to lunch, be nice to the wait staff. She's watching.

- **Assume nothing.**

Don't assume a woman has a husband. Don't assume she has kids. Don't assume she's not the decision maker. Don't assume anything. Women wield the purchasing power. Even in cases when they're not writing the checks themselves, they are the influencers who make things happen. This is an especially important point to remember with young women, who have more disposable income than ever before, and larger responsibilities at work than women of previous generations had at the same age.

- **Cater to kids when you can.**

If a woman's children are happy and occupied, she can focus on her conversation with you. If they're miserable, so is she. Whether you use toys, videos, or coloring books, find ways to incorporate the "kid factor" into your environment so that Mom can concentrate on whatever it is you're selling.

- **Use compliments.**

Women compliment each other constantly. It's an important part of American female culture. In sales situations, compliment her good judgment, good taste, or great questions. Fair or not, it's generally acceptable for a female salesperson to compliment another woman's personal appearance. However, this is dangerous territory for men and best avoided. "I actually had a copier salesman tell me to put my pretty little hand on the "start" button once," says Christine, a marketing executive. "I was so furious I switched vendors."

- **Disclose your own vulnerability.**

Acknowledge when a purchasing decision is difficult. Saying something like "I remember the first time I bought my own hard drive—I didn't know where to begin" will be appreciated and make her feel good that you're helping her. This kind of affirmation is a critical part of the way that women talk to one another. The "geniuses" at Apple are really good at this.

- **Acknowledge her male partner when selling to couples.**

Women tend to be sensitive about making sure their men look good in front of others, especially when they earn high incomes or make more money than their partners. It's important to make sure a woman's husband or male partner is made to feel important and included in the sales process, even if she is clearly the decision maker. Understand that she may be saying little during the transaction because she doesn't want to inadvertently emasculate her husband.

- **Don't assume a nod means yes.**

Women and men have different reasons for nodding. Men nod to show agreement; women nod to demonstrate that they're listening. Women's nods can mean, *Yes, go on, I understand.* They don't necessarily mean, *Yes, I'm ready for you to close this sale.* Women often nod vigorously when they're in conversation with one another. Watch for the cues and don't try to close too fast, or you'll risk turning her off with what she thinks is a hard sell.

- **Lead with the emotional, close with the rational.**

This is particularly true for luxury products, where the need to buy is purely an emotional one. Women need help justifying a major purchase more than men do. Help her rationalize the decision so there are no guilt feelings about spending money on herself. When it comes to shopping, guilt is largely a female issue, probably because men buy more products based on need and women buy more products based on want.

- **Discuss service and maintenance policies.**

Don't skimp on this information, because as we've seen, women will fast-forward to the worst-case scenario and want to know what their options are should things go wrong. Trust and peace of mind can be your competitive advantage.

- **Give her a reason to tell her friends or colleagues about you.**

Women are a great source of referrals. Give her something to pass along to her friends so that they can get a discount on your product or service. At a minimum, ask her if there's anyone she knows who might also be in need of whatever you're selling. If she likes you, she'll want to help you succeed.

Men Are from Mars, Women Are from Lexus

THE stereotype of the bad car salesman is so ingrained in our collective psyche that car buying remains the poster child for bad selling, especially with women. It's shocking that the second-biggest purchase most people will ever make, after buying a home, is a transaction they dread. People love cars; most just hate what they have to go through to get one. Interestingly, 92 percent of the industry's salespeople are men,[1] even though the majority of new car sales are driven (forgive the pun) by women.

From the standpoint of good selling techniques, the industry is not without its bright spots. Toyota's Lexus brand is one of them. Slightly more than half (51 percent) of all Lexus buyers are women, and just twenty years after its introduction in the United States, the brand has the highest customer retention rate of any luxury car. Fully 60 percent of Lexus owners trade in their old Lexus for a new one.[2]

Talk to a woman about her Lexus and you'll want to find a comfortable chair, because you may be there for a while. I asked Louise, a single, sixty-five-year-old businesswoman who's owned three consecutive Lexuses, why she likes the brand so much. "Do you have half an hour?" was her response. She and the other Lexus buyers I interviewed were impressive in their devotion. But after speaking to them at length, it became clear that these women weren't just talking about their cars—they were talking about their *relationship* with Lexus.

"I don't think it's product that draws women to Lexus," says Nancy Fein, the vice president of customer relations at Toyota, who has spent years working with the Lexus brand.

"There are lots of competitive products that could be considered equally attractive. The biggest issue for women is the whole aspect of service, from the sales experience to customer service." And when it comes to delivering an experience that women want, Lexus has cracked the code.

Setting the stage

First and foremost, Lexus sets the stage for effective selling. Good salesmanship is like great theater—it requires the right props, the right script, and the right setting. It sounds so simple, but creating a beautiful atmosphere is important for getting women in the mind-set to spend money— especially on a $50,000 (or more) car. Lexus works with its dealers to set high standards for ambience, because it understands that the comfort of the dealership is the first part of women's experience with the brand.

Lexus dealerships typically feature designer furniture, soft lighting, and the kinds of amenities you might expect from a luxury hotel lobby. Premium coffee, flat-screen televisions, and upscale baked goods all create the kind of vibe that's designed to make customers want to linger. One of the dealerships in Chicago, called McGrath, actually has a full café right in the middle of the place, where about a dozen customers were relaxing and sipping hot coffees as I walked by.

When it comes to buying expensive things, women like to be romanced during the sales process. This romancing isn't sexual, of course—in this context, the word describes an atmosphere that makes women excited and filled with anticipation about what they're going to buy. For many people, buying a new car is one of the most thrilling moments in their lives. The fact that this is not reflected at most dealerships is one of the biggest missed opportunities in the history of missed opportunities. Getting the keys to a new car should have all the excitement of a wedding day. After all, some people stick with their cars longer than with their marriages.

Seeing the sales process through female eyes

After hearing so many glowing reviews of the Lexus sales experience, I decided to test it out myself. When I mystery-shopped the expansive McGrath Lexus dealership in Chicago, I noticed virtually everything about the process—like a typical woman. If you haven't studied women's reactions to your own sales environment, you should. Here's how it works. As soon as the salesman introduced himself, I sized him up to determine whether I could trust him. My first clue was his language—was he polite, and did he use good grammar? Yes and yes. Was he respectful? Yes again. He made no comments about the fact that I was a woman on my own at a car dealership. He didn't look me up and down. He asked me all kinds of relevant and appropriate questions about my lifestyle, and what was important to me in a car. Then, as we strode through the place, I measured the reactions of his colleagues. Was my salesperson a respected member of the team, or did I get a dud? I searched their faces and body language for clues. Most people want to be sold by someone who appears to be successful, because it makes them more confident in their buying decision.

Then I checked out what the other salespeople were doing—were they busy and businesslike, or just hanging out

making small talk? Were they making fun of previous customers? I strained to hear. Walking past them, I wondered,
were they looking at me like—"He's got a live one!"—or did
they seem respectful? Upon inspection, they all came across
as professional. They smiled and nodded as I walked by. And
just like the scene in the movie *Fargo,* where police chief
Marge Gunderson discovers clues to a crime by observing
the notes on sales manager Jerry Lundegaard's desk, I found
myself reading the notes and pieces of paper in my salesperson's tidy cubicle. Nothing incriminating.

All of that inspection took place within the first three
minutes of meeting the salesman. He passed with flying
colors. Then he casually mentioned that if I purchased a car,
I would receive free car washes at the dealership, and that
once a week a massage therapist would be able to give me a
complimentary massage while my car was being washed.
The mere mention of the word "massage" during the sales
pitch seemed to lower my blood pressure several points
(along with my defenses) and suddenly made me feel all
warm and fuzzy about Lexus. In spite of myself, I began to
sense that being a Lexus owner would give me entrée to a
certain *lifestyle,* not just a car. Suddenly I had visions of becoming the kind of person who got weekly massages and
drove a spotlessly clean luxury car.

Mastering the sale

Setting the stage for the sale is part one. Selling the actual
product is part deux. Lexus has different levels of internal
sales-training certification on everything from product
knowledge to customer handling. All Lexus salespeople are

scored on customer satisfaction, and those who meet the highest levels of certification are called "master certified." When a salesperson reaches this level, the company subsidizes a car lease for his or her own personal Lexus. It's a perk that helps the company retain its best and most experienced people.

Louise, the three-time Lexus owner, is proof that the system works. "I've used the same salesman for all three of my Lexuses," she says. "And he drives a Lexus himself, so he knows the car. But one of the best things about dealing with him, and with Lexus, is that you don't have to hassle and play all those silly games to buy your car. Women don't like that. We're intelligent and we don't want our time wasted. For me, buying from Lexus is a stress-free experience." Louise is not only loyal to the brand; she's loyal to her specific salesperson. To her, he is as much a part of the brand as the car itself.

My salesperson at Lexus clearly had been trained in customer etiquette, which is an important aspect of selling to female buyers. "Women are more interested in manners," says Annette Sykora, who runs two car dealerships in Texas, in addition to her role as chairman of the National Automotive Dealers Association. "They like the pleases and the thank you's and the yes ma'ams. It matters more to them; my men customers don't really care."

The salesman I dealt with not only had good manners, he shrewdly leveraged Lexus' third-party credibility, which was compelling. On his desk was a binder of J. D. Power & Associates survey statistics, and stacks of articles praising Lexus' performance in media ranging from *BusinessWeek* to the *Financial Times*. His attitude was, "Don't take my word for it—see what these respected publications have to say," which is an effective technique for persuading women to believe in a product, especially when it's expensive and they could use the reassurance.

Service is the sweet spot for Lexus

Lexus sets the stage well for selling, and they train their salespeople to negotiate in an effective but low-pressure manner. Their final stroke of business acumen is to provide outstanding service after the sale. Lexus views each sale as the beginning of its relationship with a customer, not the end. This is the way the company has built its position as the luxury-category leader in customer loyalty. Every Lexus comes with a warranty that has female appeal written all over it. The company provides free, 24/7 roadside assistance; a bumper-to-bumper warranty; free loaner cars when a vehicle comes in for service; free car washes; and new-owner events in which customers can get help doing those pesky-but-necessary things like installing Bluetooth and changing automatic settings on seats and radios.

Lexus' roadside assistance program is the star attraction of the company's service offerings. The American Automobile Association (AAA) backs up the program, though fully 65 percent of the calls are responded to by Lexus dealers. "We give the dealer the first opportunity to answer a call for help, and most dealers will take the calls for their own customers during normal business hours," says Fein. A dealer who responds to a call for roadside assistance typically sends out a truck with the dealership's name on the door, along with one of their own technicians. The dealership effectively becomes a bit of a hero every time a customer sees its branded truck coming down the street to rescue them.

This is one of the reasons women describe a relationship with Lexus that goes beyond their cars. Safety is critical to women. There are few things they dread more than the thought of being broken down alone on the side of the road at night, or worse—being broken down with their children. "If a man breaks down it would be inconvenient; if a woman breaks down it could be life threatening," says Courtney Caldwell, editor in chief of *Road & Travel* magazine. Given that point of view, it's easy to see how this kind of service after the sale keeps women coming back. "Lexus is a reliable car, but the service process takes care of you," says Fein. "It feels like someone's watching out for you. And the men like it, too."

When women are on the receiving end of this kind of treatment, they tell their friends, and friends of friends. "I've told so many people about my great experiences that now every time my book club meets, it looks like a Lexus parking lot," says Louise. Toyota's Fein is matter-of-fact about why. "When you get right down to it, the only thing that makes Lexus different is our value system," she says. The company has a covenant that states, *Lexus will treat each customer as we would a guest in our own home.* Each dealer commits to follow it. "The Lexus covenant is a powerful shared value within the organization," says Fein. "Anyone can build a building. Anyone can develop a training program. Anyone can copy what you're doing, but they can't copy the way you do it."

Lessons for your business

Takeaways from Lexus include:

- **Set the stage for success.**

Women need to feel comfortable before they buy—especially when spending large amounts of money. Put them in the right frame of mind to respond to your sales pitch through the way you decorate and light your sales environment; the way you train and retain your salespeople; and the way customers are treated from the moment they walk in the door. These elements are all a part of the ambience "package" a woman notices about your business. Leverage the tips in this chapter and be creative. Whatever small amount of money McGrath Lexus spends on a weekly massage therapist is worth its weight in gold in terms of customer perception, brand allegiance, and talk value.

- **Address your customers' biggest fear, and turn it into a competitive advantage.**

Lexus has addressed women's concerns about safety with a 24/7 roadside assistance program that comes with every new or certified preowned car. Sure, the company builds safe cars, but it goes one step further by saying, "Even if the worst-case scenario happens with our cars, we'll be there." Take a look at your own industry. What's the worst-case scenario for your own customers, and how can you address it more effectively? Better yet, how can you turn this into an advantage by dealing with it directly? You probably have a service guarantee or a warranty program, but the marketing value inherent within it may be lying untapped. Look at ways to leverage it instead.

- **A great sales experience is only as good as the product behind it.**

Lexus is praised by women for its service, but that wouldn't mean a thing if its cars weren't high quality. In any business, no amount of great salesmanship can make up for a lousy product.

Super Store or Super Snore?
Selling Through the Retail Environment

WHEN it comes to selling just about anything outside of fishing rods, orienting your retail environment for the female consumer is a must. It's true that young men are being encouraged to shop more these days and to take a greater interest in things like grooming and fashion. But once they get married, men still tend to abdicate shopping responsibilities to their other half, and soon their shopping muscles go slack. It appears that men take the strongest interest in fashion and grooming when sex is at stake; after the wedding day, they no longer lurk around Abercrombie & Fitch in such large numbers.

The widespread acceptance of online shopping is forcing brick-and-mortar retail to develop in two distinct ways. First, it must provide the human touch and sensory experience that's impossible to get online; second, it must be efficient enough for people to feel they can get in and out of the stores as quickly as they'd like. The imperative, in essence, is to give people something special in the store that they can't get in the virtual world. I went looking to find the companies that do it best, and what I found was a nirvana for little girls.

A city inside a store: American Girl

The American Girl store is a paragon of retailing that's so over the top with wholesome characters and experiences, it makes the average department store seem like a funeral parlor. At the Chicago location, it was hard to tell who was more excited, the moms and grandmothers or the young girls. The store is a blur of happy mayhem and mother/daughter/grandmother bonding. The day of my visit, the song "Come On, Get Happy" by the Partridge Family blared out into the street at top volume, ostensibly to lure in more customers. This was clearly unnecessary, as there's often a line of people who come from all over the Midwest to shop here. As they say in retail parlance, American Girl is a *destination* shopping experience. It also may be a foreshadowing of things to come.

The more time we spend online or in front of television and video screens, the less time there is to engage with other people in the tactile and ancient ritual of shopping at markets and brick-and-mortar stores. A sensory explosion such as the American Girl store is the antidote to the flatness and solitude of online shopping, and it just may hold the key to survival for the next generation of retail.

At its most fundamental, the American Girl store sells dolls. Yet it has transformed every conceivable aspect of a girl's relationship with her doll into an experience. There's a hair salon inside the store where little girls jostle to get their doll's hair styled just like their own. There's a doll hospital down the hallway from the salon, where a crackerjack team of "nurses" and "doctors" fix doll injuries, including everything from a general cleaning to "major surgery." There's even a museumlike series of vignettes, with craftsmanship worthy of the Smithsonian Institution, depicting the imaginary lives and historical backgrounds of each doll in the American Girl brand family. These vignettes make visitors feel that the American Girl retail experience is actually educational and not just entertaining.

Each doll has a theme based on a different period in American history. Addy, for example, is an African American girl growing up during the Civil War. Julia is from the 1970s, wearing bell bottoms and struggling with her parents' divorce. Kit Kittredge is an aspiring young journalist from the Depression era; the character made the transition from American Girl doll to movie star in 2008, when a hit movie—with a real human actress (Abigail Breslin)—was made about her. Each doll comes with its own life story of pluck, courage, and integrity, neatly packaged into an accompanying book. American Girl has sold so many of these books that it's now one of the top children's book publishers in the United States.[3]

To capture the memories of their shopping trip forever, there's a photography studio where girls can get a photo taken of themselves and their dolls on a mocked-up cover of *American Girl* magazine (which is actually a real magazine), ready to take home in just fifteen minutes. And when they've worked up an appetite from the unbridled capitalism of it all, there's a bistro with real waiters and waitresses, serving children and their mothers real food, like Chicken Paillard and Grilled Pacific King Salmon, with a real bill at the end. The dolls sit at the tables on special booster seats. They have their own menu.

The cost for the dolls? About $100 each. The cost for lunch? About $20 per person. The cost for a photo package?

About $30. The emotional rewards for all this mother-daughter bonding? Priceless.

The American Girl store is clearly designed to connect with both the younger set *and* their mothers, who are the ones paying for all of these products and experiences. It represents a new way of thinking about retail, and gives a powerful example of what it can offer that the online world can't. When it's done right, retail can provide a vivid, tactile experience. It can offer personalized service that makes someone feel special. It can offer smells, sounds, and sights that stoke the imagination. It can bring people together. It can leave shoppers with an indelible, emotionally charged memory that makes them want to return again and again. Currently, there are few retailers that fit this bill, but competition from the online world and from game changers such as American Girl may change all that. For the industry to survive, it's worth examining all the different factors that go into creating a retail environment that women will want to participate in again and again.

Principles of Female-Friendly Retail

RESEARCH shows that creating positive emotional experiences for shoppers increases consumer spending and involvement. No surprise there. But in most categories, people aren't given a positive emotional experience, and when that happens, it affects the entire industry, because at that point people tend to default to the retailer that offers the lowest price.

Women have always viewed shopping as a social experience. Perhaps it's a hangover from stone-age times, when women spent their days gathering food alongside female clan members as well as their own kids. Whatever the reason, a day spent shopping with girlfriends is still the definition of a great day out for many women the world over. In our time-starved society, those days are now typically relegated to weekends or special occasions, and when women are not with their friends, shopping often becomes an exercise in efficiency: get in, get out, get home, and check a few more things off the list. "Retail is a reflection of life," says Stephen Hoch, professor of marketing and director of the Baker Retailing Initiative at the University of Pennsylvania's Wharton School. "Whatever changes are happening in society are going to be reflected in retail."

How to get women to linger, enjoy the experience, and buy more products comes down to the following principles.

- **Friendly, available help matters.**

In the online world, if someone can't find something they're looking for, they immediately go to another website or click on a different link. Either way, they usually get immediate gratification. This has changed our frame of reference, and it means that when women have to wander around a store looking for help, five minutes can feel like five hours. One of the smartest guys I know, Chris Gray of the shopper marketing agency Saatchi & Saatchi X, puts it this way: "When it comes to women shoppers, a lack of humans can put a retailer in a dangerous position."

- **Women have a kill-several-birds-with-one-stone shopping approach.**

With their multitasking mindset (as opposed to men's

linear style of thinking), women have a tendency to group errands together to maximize productivity. This makes them open to picking up products that weren't on their list, because buying something now will save them a trip back later (or so they will tell themselves), and besides, they always have their antennae out for things that members of their "Broadway cast" might like.

A more academic way to say it is that women shop in a *holistic* fashion. Niketown and IKEA are two major retailers that provide great examples of how to place products together in vignettes. Women love seeing how outfits and rooms come together, and these companies do a stellar job of packaging individual components into bigger packages. These vignettes not only spark customers' fantasies about how a particular look might work for them but are viewed as a great time saver, because someone has done the coordination work for them.

- **Women's shopping experiences are transformed when children are involved.**

More than ever, kids, strollers, child carriers, and other accoutrements come with women on their shopping trips. How easy is your retail environment to navigate, given this reality? From family bathrooms at the store entrance (to take care of the inevitable before families start shopping) to dressing rooms that accommodate children (doors that go all the way down to the floor so that they can't run out) and aisles wide enough for strollers, kids are an important reality for almost anyone with a predominantly female shopping base. This makes it just plain silly that we still have a six-items-or-less policy for so many dressing rooms. It limits sales because people are so time-crunched they don't want to make multiple trips to a dressing room—especially when there is no one there to help them get different sizes anyway.

- **Women will abandon a personal shopping experience if it inconveniences their companions.**

Few retailers invest in the simplest of products: chairs for weary shoppers and the people accompanying them. More clothes have been abandoned in more dressing rooms because a woman can hear the audible sighs and distress calls of her (often male) companion, propped up against a pillar in the ladies' department. Simple furnishings, such as chairs and magazines, can make all the difference between whether a shopping trip is cut off after an hour or lasts the whole day. My local Nordstrom has an entertainment "pit" outside the ladies' dressing room where people (mainly men, from my experience) can relax on a giant couch and watch movies while their female companions try on clothes.

There are an infinite number of ways to unearth female-friendly insights within a retail environment. More mirrors are needed everywhere, especially in purse and shoe departments. Those little ones on the stools will not do, and yes, women need a mirror to "try on" a purse. All that's needed is a genuine desire to understand, and the answers will be there for the taking.

lululemon athletica: The "Un-retailer"

LULULEMON athletica is one of my favorite stores. If you haven't heard of it yet, you will: it is one of the fastest-growing athletic apparel companies in the world, with about a hundred locations in Canada, the United States, and Australia. In 2008, *BusinessWeek* named this yoga-focused retailer number two on its list of the top fifty hot-growth companies. Based in Vancouver, Canada, and founded by a surfer turned yoga practitioner, the company's vision is bolder than you'd expect from an athletic retailer: "Elevating the world from mediocrity to greatness." The lululemon vision translates not only to the company's beautiful and technically brilliant athletic apparel, but also to its retailing practices. "It's the best growth story in retail today," said Paul Lejuez, a senior analyst at Credit Suisse.[4]

You don't have to love yoga to love lululemon. I don't know a downward dog from an upward cat, and I can't resist the place. It's a bit like Williams-Sonoma in that way—you don't have to cook to lust after the products sold there. What makes lululemon different is that each store feels like a small, locally owned boutique, so much that customers are often shocked to find out there's more than one location. (They're even more devastated to find out it's a chain.) The company's commitment to the local communities surrounding its stores is palpable and present in every store. And who is lululemon trying to target with its community focus? You guessed it.

"Women aren't just the future, they're the now," says the company's founder and chairman, Chip Wilson, an entrepreneur who founded a surf, skate, and snowboard company prior to starting lululemon. He explains his vision of lululemon stores this way: "I see a lot of U.S. retail as schlocky and fake and not real, and catering to the lowest common denominator. I didn't have any experience in retail when I started out, so I had to invent it myself. I thought, *What would I want if I were the customer?* How do I take a chain store and not make it a chain store? "

The answer is what you see today if you walk into any lululemon store. Here's what you'll find:

- **Pictures of local people on its walls.**
  Each store is decorated with pictures of local yoga practitioners, athletes, runners, and dancers striking poses in photogenic places around town. Next to the dressing rooms, a collection of bulletin boards features information about local yoga classes, local instructors who are the company's "ambassadors," and the names and interests of the lululemon employees who work in that particular store. The ambassadors are a key to the company's retail strategy. Before it opens in a new market, lululemon spends months approaching local yoga studios and their influential instructors, and gives them clothing in exchange for feedback on the fit and designs. As a result, every influential yoga person in town is spotted wearing lululemon, not only in the street but also in the photos on the stores' walls.

- **The salespeople are athletes.**
  lululemon hires athletes and yoga practitioners who, in their words, "have a life outside of work." Instead of spending money on marketing (lululemon does no traditional mass-market advertising, nor does it advertise sales of any kind), it plows its money into employee training.

"I believe in the law of attraction," says Chip. "If you bring great people in, they'll attract other great people, and the business will take care of itself."

- **They call you by name.**

Each dressing room features an erasable whiteboard on the outside of the door, where the lululemon salesperson writes down your name—and even asks how to spell it properly. For the rest of the time you're trying on clothes, you hear someone calling out your name to ask if you need help. It's a simple but impressive technique. The stores also feature seating for the shopper's companions.

- **They promote their vision.**

lululemon prominently displays the company's manifesto on the wall of its stores, including nuggets such as "Dance, sing, floss, and travel," and "Your outlook on life is a direct reflection of how much you like yourself." The manifesto is also printed on lululemon's bags, which are so popular they were featured on the front page of the *New York Times* as a fashion trend.

- **They offer free on-site tailoring of your purchases.**

Not only is this something that's extremely rare in women's mass-market apparel, it's all but unheard of in the sports apparel category.

- **They ask for your feedback and prominently display it.**

There's a chalkboard asking for comments on the fit and sizing of lululemon products. Customers are invited to post their thoughts publicly.

- **They host free yoga classes every weekend.**
Classes are usually held at the stores and are free and open to everyone. lululemon says that its mission is to introduce more people to the benefits of yoga any way it can, and when you're out under a tree with staff members learning how to do a sun salutation, you believe it.

Eric Petersen, one of the company's senior executives, sums up the retail experience this way: "It's the small things that matter. This is why we have an amazing guest experience. We care about people's communities, not just the media in those communities. The things we do are so simple and so primitive, and yet everyone else overlooks them. It's really easy. We hire passionate people and we listen to what they and our guests have to say. We're engaged in a continuous conversation. That's it."

Lessons for your business

Takeaways from lululemon include:

- **Employees can be your greatest form of advertising.**
lululemon does no mass-market advertising and never has. Yet it's a top hot-growth company. It's done this by investing money in the people it hires and the products it creates.

- **Wooing local influencers pays off.**
Before it opens one of its stores, lululemon spends months creating relationships with influential yoga practitioners and athletes in the area, who help spread the word about the company's imminent store opening and provide vital third-party credibility for its products.

- **Personalization doesn't have to be expensive or high-tech.**

The simple whiteboards on the dressing room doors of each store allow employees to address the customers inside by name. Being helped in this way in a retail environment is something so unexpected that it floors customers and makes them feel great about buying from "their" lululemon store.

A Tangled Web: Selling to Women Online

How many principles of great retailing translate online? The answer is most of them, and then some. Understanding what women want in e-commerce is critical because women outshop men across most major consumer categories online, just as they do in traditional retail outlets.[5] It's women who are driving the growth of retail innovations like local- and groupbuying sites, flash-sale sites, and digital couponing. When you consider that the e-commerce market in the United States alone generated more than $227 billion in sales during 2010, there are literally billions of reasons to make women happy online.[6]

Women's behavior online tends to mimic their offline behavior. They window-shop, chat with friends, hunt for deals, ask like-minded people their opinions, and look for a pleasant, convenient, and even inspiring shopping experience. They do a tremendous amount of product research online, which wasn't as possible back in the days before the Internet, when they had to rip out pages from magazines and stick them in a drawer or file folder.

Ever the errand consolidators, women view online shopping as an important tool in their multitasking arsenals, and women at every age and life stage are drawn to its convenience. For mothers of young children, it offers extraordinary advantages. This is easy to understand if you've ever escorted a posse of small children to Target. How nice it must be to put the kids to bed, pour a glass of cabernet, turn on the TV, and go to Target.com instead. The benefits of online shopping are beyond what anyone could have imagined ten years ago. The Internet is even turning women into online merchants themselves. Who needs to host a garage sale when you can get rid of that old couch on Craigslist or eBay instead?

There are some important considerations when it comes to appealing to women online. Even today, buying products on the Internet is viewed as riskier than buying them in a store.[7] People still worry about the confidentiality of their credit card information, and this is especially true for women. If you're a small business that's not widely known, making your financial privacy policies known is crucial.

Studies show that the number one complaint of people shopping online is that the item they received didn't look like it did online.[8] For women, that means they have to return it, and that's an inconvenience, no matter how liberal the return policy. This is where a good zoom feature becomes critical. If a retailer is showcasing a purse, for example, it should be shown from every angle, including the inside, so that women can see what the lining looks like and whether or not the product has interior pockets. Women need this level of detail to feel confident in buying something they can't inspect for themselves.

The website Sears.com does the zoom function one better through its "My Virtual Model" feature. The site allows shoppers to input their height, weight, and personal characteristics—even a photo of themselves—to create their own animated online model to try on clothing. It also offers the same feature for the home fashions section of the site, enabling shoppers to click and paste everything from furniture to paint colors in images of rooms. It's brilliant and totally unexpected.

The second biggest online shopping complaint is not being able to talk to a live person about purchasing questions or concerns.[9] Some websites hide their 800 numbers as if they were plutonium, and that kind of poor customer service is simply unacceptable. Post it prominently on the home page of your website, as Nordstrom does, and cater to different preferences by offering every type of customer service technology you can afford, from live chat to e-mail.

Principles of female-friendly e-commerce sites

Broadly speaking, women like to feel smart about purchases they've made online, they like to feel good about the companies they've bought from, and they like to feel proud that they're such savvy shoppers. In other words, they want the same outcome they seek in the offline world of retail, but with dramatically more convenience. The following are some tactical ways to achieve this on the Internet.

- **Women like being involved in clubs and membership programs that let them hear about new products and discounts before anyone else.**
  Who doesn't like to be part of the in-crowd? Exclusive access to time-sensitive offers is the appeal of invitation-only businesses like Gilt Groupe and the growing number of flash-sale and sample-sale sites around the world. Check out Internet darling DailyCandy (and its sister

sample site, Swirl) to see one of the Web's true pioneers in creating female appeal. DailyCandy set the gold standard for delivering messages to women with a wink, a *pssst,* and copy that consistently makes them feel like they're in on something special.

- **Women like websites that recommend matching products when they select an item.**

This is an incredibly powerful way to upsell, for every single category out there. (Would you like birdseed with that bird feeder?) Offering recommendations simply mimics what great salespeople do in brick-and-mortar stores: they suggest items they think you would like, based on knowledge of your past preferences. Amazon is the king of recommendations, which are a helpful tool for women in any category. As we've discussed in this chapter, women think holistically and like to kill several birds with one stone, so they'll appreciate being able to look at recommendations that will save them time and make their shopping experience more productive. It's a modern way to deliver old-fashioned service.

- **Women like to know what other people are buying.**

Women's fashion trends change exponentially faster than men's. My dad wore what seemed to be the same pair of khaki pants for twenty years. Flag what's trendy and popular in clever ways, like the way Target.com sometimes uses the label "Best Seller" as a euphemism for "this is what everybody else is buying." In any category, women are interested in knowing what the hot or popular items are. Increasingly, retailers are leveraging

Facebook to showcase items to customers that their friends have "liked."

- **Buying gifts online has been the greatest boon for women since the invention of the wheel.**

Women like to shop for gifts online because the stakes are so much lower than buying products for themselves— you never have to try on a gift—and the shipping is a beautiful thing. Your website should help women in their gift-giving quest by flagging age-appropriate, gender-appropriate gifts in clear language (if she doesn't have kids, how does she know what an eight-year-old boy might want?) and, of course, offering low-cost or free gift wrapping. Starbucks.com does something clever— it gives people the ability to personalize its Starbucks gift cards online for almost any occasion, complete with a custom message right on the card, like "Happy 25th Birthday, Sam." At last, the impersonal gift card has been personalized, by the clever folks at Starbucks.

- **Women like a "clean" Web environment.**

The study of female design preferences is a new one and deserves to be taken seriously. New research from the U.K. indicates that women are drawn to bright colors, rounded lines, 2-D representation of objects, and patterned or detailed surfaces.[10] In a world where there are relatively few female Web designers, it's important to conduct usability testing with women. Too much clutter online, for example, can make women shut down. It might be exciting to look through a messy sale table at a store, just in case there's a great find underneath, but there are few equivalents for this online. A good keyword search engine for your website is critical. Women notice everything, and when there's too much to notice, they can get information overload and abandon ship, especially when they're not tech savvy.

- **A website's return policy can make or break a deal.**

Most women barely have enough time to buy a product, let alone return it. The websites with the most generous return policies—like Zappos.com—are often the most successful. "My favorite shopping websites tend to be online versions of brick-and-mortar stores, as long as I can make a return at the store," says Leslie, a public relations executive. "I absolutely hate having to hassle with the post office to send something back, and I hate having to pay to ship it back." The success of the Zappos online shoe business has been driven in large part by the goodwill generated through the company's generous return policies.

- **Overcommunicate after the sale.**

Give her an order confirmation number as soon as she's paid; send a confirmation immediately to her e-mail address; let her know when the product has shipped; ask her how her experience was after she's received it. These are all steps that will make women feel more comfortable about sending you their precious financial information online again.

- **Close more sales by featuring time-sensitive offers.**

Women do a lot of browsing online. Convert window shoppers to buyers by offering the same kind of time-sensitive sales that exist in the offline world. Most people need a sense of urgency to buy something, especially if it's something they don't actually need. Flash-sale sites leverage this concept on a daily basis, often complete with countdown clocks. For a tutorial on how to generate excitement through time-sensitive offers, study sites like Groupon, RueLaLa, Living Social, and Vente-Privee.

- **Include a "share" mechanism.**

Women are the world's biggest drivers of word-of-mouth publicity, and as you know by now, they are always thinking about the needs of other people in their lives. Enabling women to send an e-mail to friends about what they've just purchased or what you're offering on sale is just the ticket to get the word spreading. This is how I found out that fashion designer Nanette Lepore had created a new line of shoes for Keds. My friend knew I was a fan of Lepore and sent me a little e-mail notice from the Keds website. As I write this, I'm wearing my new polka-dot flip-flops from the line.

As DailyCandy CEO Dany Levy says, "Sometimes it's okay to say something as short and simple as 'Hey, look at this—it's kind of neat!'" And she should know; it's the foundation of her very successful, female-focused business, which was sold to Comcast for $125 million in 2008.[11]

7

WE HAVE SEEN

THE FUTURE,

AND IT IS FEMALE

Applying the Knowledge to Your Business

Considering that women make up more than half the population (51 percent), is it even possible to consider them a business "category," when their numbers are so large? When they range from urban Latinas to small-town moms, span the age gamut from millennials to boomers, and live in places as different as Muncie and Mumbai? It's an important question, and the answer is this: *women around the world are more similar than they are different.*

As we've seen throughout these pages, women are united by their brain structures, hormone levels, and biological role in birthing the human race. They also are united by their roles as caregivers, relationship builders, and keepers of the peace. Women talk about the same topics the world over—their feelings, their families, their social issues, their latest shopping finds, their bodies, their jobs, their plans for the weekend, and their hopes for the future.

While there is no disputing the importance of customer segmentation, which could be the subject for a different book entirely, these similarities mean that the ideas on which this book is based can be used wherever women live and work. The success of multinationals such as Procter & Gamble, MasterCard, and Unilever, which market their products to women in every corner of the globe—often through the same umbrella marketing campaigns customized for local markets—prove the validity of this concept. Yet it would be foolish to suggest that women are one large, homogeneous group. Cultural context is critical. No one would pitch a product in Los Angeles in the same way they would in Riyadh, nor would they pitch a product to an elderly woman in the same manner as to a teenager. Leveraging universal female traits, in combination with cultural context and life stage, is the one-two-three punch for winning women consumers.

There is no doubt; women's consumer domination is here for the long term. The global trends driving women's educational attainment, workforce participation, and purchasing patterns mean that women are expected to drive the consumer economy for the next twenty-five years or longer. As you begin the process of catering to the alpha consumer, keep in mind the new paradigm of the female-consumer world order.

The Top Ten Rules to Remember About Women Consumers

1. Women buy or influence the purchase of most consumer products.

2. Gender is the most powerful determinant of how a person views the world and everything in it. It's more powerful than age, income, race, or geography.

3. Women's brain structures and hormone levels are different from men's, and women are raised in an unseen gender culture that shapes their priorities and worldviews in ways that can be imperceptible to men.

4. Female culture should be studied with the same focus that entering a foreign market requires. Mastering female culture is the key to success for companies that depend on women consumers.

5. The person who makes a sales transaction isn't necessarily the decision maker. Even if the woman of the house does not earn a paycheck, she likely determines her household's expenditures.

6. Pink is not a strategy.

7. If women make up a significant portion of your customer base, they should be represented proportionately on your management team.

8. There are five important trends driving the world's female population that should be considered when making long-term planning decisions for your business.

9. Women around the world are more similar than they are different.

10. When you please women, you tend to make your male customers happier, too.

Whether you're male or female, you can learn the most important drivers of the world's alpha consumers and apply these insights to your business.

"The greatest thing I've learned is that if you're a man, you have to create a filter that overrides your own natural responses as a male, or as a businessperson in an industry that's traditionally skewed male," says Ryland Homes' Eric Elder, who spends a great deal of his time studying women home buyers. "Your filter needs to be made up of real facts on how the female segment functions in your business, not stereotypes. I tell my colleagues that I'm not trying to understand women just to be nice; I'm doing it because they're the ones who write the checks."

How to Begin

At this point, you may feel enthusiasm for creating a more female-focused organization, but you'll likely need the participation of your colleagues to accomplish this internally. The steps outlined in the pages ahead can help you begin the process.

First, the diagnosis. The following framework will help you determine the "female literacy" of your company. Stage 4 is the most sophisticated; Stage 1 is the least.

BUSINESS FOCUS	STAGE 1
Customer Knowledge	No data on female/male customer split
Customer Service	No data on gender split of customer service inquiries
Sales Training	No gender-specific training initiatives for sales employees
Marketing and Sales Strategic Leadership	No women in marketing and sales leadership positions No on-the-job gender education
Product Development Leadership	No women in product development/design leadership Human factors engineering does not include female factors engineering
Ad Agency Creative Execution	No women on creative team for clients targeting women, no training on gender education

STAGE 2	STAGE 3	STAGE 4
Baseline knowledge of female/male customer split	Clear understanding of gender split and whether company's share of women's market is going up or down	Corporate culture aligned around a predominantly female customer base
General sense that women are lead callers/inquirers but no specific initiatives to address this	Consistent data collection on gender split in customer service inquiries and customer loyalty	Education of call center employees to address dynamics of gender; customer service experience in sync with marketing messages
Informal acknowl-edgment that sales techniques may be modified based on whether prospect is male or female	Formal training/ education to address gender differences	Formal sales training for employees of both genders to address women's communication styles
Junior-level women in marketing and sales positions	Senior-level women in marketing and sales positions Education for staff on gender differences	Management-level women in marketing and sales positions, and training for all staff members on gender differences
Junior-level women in product development/design Some female factors testing	Senior-level women in product development/design Female factors testing and in-depth research with women	Management-level women in product development/design, and ethnographic research programs with women
Junior-level women on creative team for clients targeting women	At least one senior-level woman on creative team for clients targeting women	Director-level woman on creative team for clients targeting women, and gender education for staff members

Once you've got a good grasp of what stage your company is in, it will become clear where to direct your efforts. When I work with companies that are at the initial stages of creating a more female-literate organization, I've found that the process outlined in the pages ahead is a realistic and practical way to begin.

STEP 1: GATHERING THE DATA

Begin by using statistics to make your case. Most important business decisions are based on data, and that means the numbers are the best and most credible place to start. Gather the data on female purchasing for your industry and determine how well your company measures up. If you have fewer women customers than the industry average, use this information to justify an audit as the first step in initiating change. If you don't collect customer data by gender, now would be a good time to start.

STEP 2: CONDUCT A MARKETING COMMUNICATIONS AUDIT

Using the principles outlined in this book, audit your company's consumer-facing communications (the simplest place to begin) to determine whether or not your marketing has female gender appeal. Review your website, advertising, public relations programming, marketing collateral, online customer reviews/blog entries, and twitter postings to determine the kind of image the company is projecting to a female audience. Use the following brief checklist as a guideline:

✔ Emotionally resonant messages about how the product will make her life better and/or improve the lives of the people she cares about

✔ Good style and design sensibility on materials and
packaging
✔ Images of people featured in materials, not just
products
✔ Messages focused on practical, helpful benefits
✔ Third-party credibility/testimonials included where
possible
✔ Socially responsible or cause marketing messaging
included
✔ Customer service/warranty messaging prominently
displayed

While it's unrealistic for all of these attributes to be reflected in one specific piece of marketing or sales material,
the list is a good reminder of what's important. When in
doubt, test with your female target.

Step 3: Conduct a Customer Service Audit

This is the step in which you determine how well the company's customer service lives up to your brand. First, find out
if your company tracks customer service inquiries by gender.
If it does, look for any significant differences in customer
feedback. If your company doesn't track inquiries by gender,
work with the customer care team to see if it might be
possible to do so. Then collaborate with colleagues or an
outside firm to "mystery-shop" your own company. Call
the 800 number; send inquiries through e-mail to see how
they're handled; visit websites to read customer opinions;
reexamine corporate return policies; go to the website
GetHuman.com to see how your company is portrayed.
(Get Human is a popular site that lists techniques for by-
passing hundreds of corporate automated-voice-response

units in order to reach a human being.) View these interactions through the lens of a busy female customer.

Step 4: Audit Your Top Three Competitors

Conduct the same marketing communications and customer service audits of your top three competitors, and then
create a master report comparing them with your own firm.
Cascade this information wide and deep, at headquarters
and in the field. In a perfect world, you'd be able to present
the information at an event in which executives' spouses are
present—like an annual meeting. This dynamic often creates great energy in the room and underscores the points
about gender differences in what ends up being a lighthearted and undeniable way. When focusing on areas ripe
for change, point out both the low-hanging fruit and the
eight-hundred-pound gorillas.

Step 5: Product Development and R&D Evaluation

Convert the product development team to your side. Talk to
them to gain a fresh understanding of how well female factors are incorporated into the product development process.
What are the current methods for gathering consumer insights? How much research is undertaken in the lab versus
in the field, closer to where consumers will actually use the
product? How many women are on the product development team?

Step 6: Sales Training

If your company has a consumer-facing sales team, find out
whether gender is addressed from a training standpoint.
Chances are it's not—and that's an area of opportunity.

The sales directors may need some convincing. To demonstrate how effective such training could be, work with a female team (either internal or external) to "mystery-shop" the sales force to determine their effectiveness with women buyers. After such an exercise, I've found that the areas for improvement are easy to identify. Armed with the results of the mystery-shopping exercise, encourage the sales team to include gender education in the training program as a tool for competitive advantage.

STEP 7: THE FIVE GLOBAL TRENDS: WHAT OPPORTUNITIES DO THEY BRING?

The global trends outlined in Chapter 3 (and the summary immediately below) can help you determine where to target your efforts and resources for the next several years. How can you leverage these trends in your long-range planning?

- ✔ More women in the workforce
- ✔ Delayed marriages, increased numbers of young singles
- ✔ Smaller families
- ✔ Divorce as a fact of life
- ✔ More older women in the world

STEP 8: MAKE YOUR CASE

Leverage the case studies and information in this book, along with your own research, to make the case for a stronger focus on understanding the culture of your female customers. Demonstrate how other industry leaders are mastering gender differences for greater profit. In my experience, this is one of the most persuasive ways to prove the opportunity.

Lobby for approval to conduct a proprietary research

project with women consumers. No matter how small the project, it's a good place to begin.

STEP 9: GET A QUICK WIN UNDER YOUR BELT

Embark on a simple, tangible project to show a quick win, to demonstrate both action and traction. This could mean anything from redrafting the look and feel of specific marketing materials to conducting a customer service training session on gender culture, or adding a women's component to current sales training efforts.

STEP 10: BENCHMARK YOUR RESULTS

Using your company's current databases, establish a benchmark that can be used to measure progress over the next several years. The benchmark could consist of information such as:

- ✔ Percentage of customers that are women
- ✔ Percentage of high-revenue customers that are women
- ✔ Customer loyalty rates by gender
- ✔ Customer service inquiries/resolutions by gender

Include gender as a consistent focus of presentations at company meetings, and continue the evangelization process until you're preaching to the converted. The future is female, and the companies that recognize and embrace this fact are the ones poised to dominate their markets. It's as simple as this: **understand women and win.**

NOTES

INTRODUCTION

1. Courtney Caldwell, editor in chief, *Road & Travel* magazine, 2009.
2. 2008 Catalyst Census of Women Corporate Officers and Top Earners of the Fortune 500.
3. Brand week data 2008 and Spencer Stuart data 2009.
4. Author's research of top one hundred U.S. ad agencies.
5. The idea of gender as cross-cultural communication was pioneered by Deborah Tannen, and Marti Barletta introduced the concept of female gender culture to the marketing world.
6. Media Metrix Worldwide Data cited in the study "Women on the Web: How Women Are Shaping the Internet," copyright ComScore, June 2010.

1: WOMEN ARE THE MOTHER LODE

1. Michael Kimmel, *The Gendered Society* (New York: Oxford University Press, 2000).
2. Ibid.
3. From imdb.com, review written by Claudio Carvalho.
4. Fortune 1000 data verified by *Fortune* magazine, 2008, and Catalyst Data, 2007.
5. Spencer Stuart research, 2009.
6. Established by author phone calls to top 100 U.S. ad agencies in 2009.
7. Catalyst Data, 2009.
8. European Parliament Committee of Women's Rights and Gender Equality, 2008, by Eva-Britt Svensson.

9. Jean Chatzky, "Earn More Than Your Man?" *Today*/MSNBC, October 1, 2007.

10. Marianne J. Legato, *Why Men Never Remember and Women Never Forget* (Emmaus, PA.: Rodale Press, 2005).

11. Pew Research Center Publications, "Women Call the Shots at Home; Public Mixed on Gender Roles in Jobs," by Rich Morin and D'Vera Cohn, September 25, 2008.

12. Cotton Incorporated, 2009.

13. Courtney Caldwell, editor in chief, *Road & Travel* magazine, 2009.

14. Consumer Electronics Association press release, April 24, 2008, also: "The Truth About Women and Consumer Electronics," 2007.

15. U.S. Department of Labor, General Facts on Women and Job-based Health, 2008.

16. *ForbesLife Executive Woman,* "The 25 Most Influential Women in Travel," by Melissa Biggs Bradley, June 30, 2008.

17. Prudential Financial, "Study on Financial Experience and Behaviors Among Women," 2004–5, and 2008–9.

18. National Association of Realtors Field Guide to Women Homebuyers, and National Association of Home Builders.

19. *Adams Wine Handbook,* 2008.

20. Electronic Software Association, "Women Comprise 40 Percent of U.S. Gamers," July 16, 2008.

2: Getting to Know the Locals

1. Daniel G. Amen, *Sex on the Brain* (New York: Three Rivers Press, 2007).

2. Marianne J. Legato, *Why Men Never Remember and Women Never Forget* (Emmaus, PA: Rodale Press, 2005), 8.

3. Amen, *Sex on the Brain,* 79.

4. Louann Brizendine, *The Female Brain* (New York: Morgan Road Books, 2006), 5.

5. Legato, *Why Men Never Remember,* 62, 72.

6. Amen, *Sex on the Brain,* 75.

7. Brizendine, *The Female Brain,* 39.

8. Legato, *Why Men Never Remember,* xvi.

9. Ibid.

10. Ibid., 13.

11. Ibid.

12. Brizendine, *The Female Brain*.

13. Deborah Tannen, *You Just Don't Understand* (New York: Quill, 1991).

14. Deborah Tannen, *Talking from 9–5* (New York: HarperCollins, 1994).

15. Tannen, *You Just Don't Understand*.

16. Ibid.

17. Study conducted in 2007 by Wharton's Jay H. Baker Retail Initiative and the Verde Group, a Toronto consulting firm.

18. Brizendine, *The Female Brain*, 37.

19. Tannen, *You Just Don't Understand*.

20. Legato, *Why Men Never Remember*, 108.

21. Ibid.

22. Ibid., 164.

23. Brizendine, *The Female Brain*, 130.

24. Ibid.

25. Diana Price, "Sexy or Sadistic? Sexist, Actually," National Organization for Women, March 19, 2007.

26. State of the American Mom Report, 2008. Marketing to Moms Coalition.

3: THE FIVE GLOBAL TRENDS DRIVING FEMALE CONSUMERS

1. "Families and Work in Transition in 12 Countries," U.S. Bureau of Labor Statistics, 2005.

2. Ibid.

3. U.S. Department of Health and Human Services Administration on Aging, with data sourced from the U.N. Department of Public Information, DP/2264, March 2002.

4. "As Layoffs Surge, Women May Pass Men in Job Force," by Catherine Rampell, *New York Times*, February 6, 2009.

5. United Nations Development Fund for Women, *The Progress of the World's Women 2005: Women, Work and Poverty*.

6. AFL-CIO Department for Professional Employees, Fact Sheet, 2006.

7. "The Importance of Sex," *Economist*, April 12, 2006.

8. Ibid.

9. Estimates are for a 1 percent annual growth rate in the U.S. female labor force, compared to 0.9 percent growth for men.

"Employment Outlook: 2004–2014—Labor Force Projections to 2014: Retiring Boomers," U.S. Bureau of Labor Statistics, November 2005.

10. "Women's Earnings and Income," Catalyst Quick Takes, 2007, citing data from 2003.

11. Kevin Daly, "Gender Equality, Growth and Global Aging," Goldman Sachs Global Economics Paper no. 154, 2007.

12. Research from BSM Media in conjunction with BlueSuitMom .com, 2004.

13. Brian Stelter, "ABC Bets 'Motherhood' Can Make a Leap from the Computer Screen," *New York Times,* May 19, 2008.

14. All age-at-first-marriage stats from 2007 *CIA World Factbook.*

15. Sam Roberts, "For Young Earners in Big City, a Gap in Women's Favor," *New York Times,* August 3, 2007 .

16. Rachel Bogardus Drew, Joint Center for Housing Studies, Harvard University, 2006.

17. Diversity Best Practices/Business Women's Network/NAFE, divisions of Working Mother Media Inc, "2007 Quick Facts: Women," 3.

18. "The Importance of Sex."

19. "Digest of Education Statistics," U.S. National Center for Education Statistics, 2005; "2007 Quick Facts: Women," 3; American Bar Association.

20. Juvenile Products Manufacturers Association press release, December 17, 2007.

21. "Facts for Features, Special Edition: 300 Million," U.S. Census Bureau data news release, August 9, 2006.

22. U.S. Census Bureau report, "Percentage of Childless Women 40–44 Years Old Increases Since 1976."

23. *CIA World Factbook,* 2009.

24. Japan Institute of Global Communications; All-China Women's Federation.

25. M. F. Brinig and D. W. Allen, " 'These Boots Are Made for Walking': Why Most Divorce Filers Are Women," *American Law and Economics Review* 2, 1 (2000): 126–69.

26. U.S. Census Bureau, 2006, as cited by Packaged Facts in the report "U.S. Singles: The New Nuclear Family."

27. Mike Stobbe, "37 Percent of U.S. Births out of Wedlock," Associated Press, November 21, 2005; Renee E. Spraggins, "We the

People: Women and Men in the United States," U.S. Census report, January 2005.

28. United Nations projections.

29. "Boomers Envisioning Retirement—How Will They Fare?" AARP news release, May 19, 2004.

30. "Beauty Comes of Age," study commissioned by Dove, a Unilever Company, September 2006.

31. "Looking at Act II of Women's Lives: Thriving and Striving from 45 On," AARP survey, April 6, 2006.

32. Jessica Wohl, "Kimberly-Clark Revamps Depend Line for Men, Women," Reuters, December 15, 2008.

33. 2007 IHRSA/American Sports Data Health Club Trend Report.

34. Data from the College Savings Foundation, 2008.

35. CDC National Center for Health Statistics Office, "Obesity Among Adults in the United States—No Statistically Significant Change Since 2003–2004," Data Brief Number 1, November 2007.

36. "Profiting from America's Portly Population," press release issued by IBISWorld research firm, PR Newswire, April 21, 2008.

37. Centers for Disease Control, "Mean Body Weight, Height, and Body Mass Index—United States, 1960–2002."

38. Data from BBC; Chinese Concern at Obesity Surge, October 12, 2004.

39. "Profiting from America's Portly Population."

40. Roopa Purushothaman, *The XX Factor,* Future Capital Holdings report, citing data from the National Sample Survey Organization.

41. Amelia Gentleman, "Indian Prime Minister Denounces Abortion of Females," *New York Times,* April 29, 2008.

42. "The Next Urban Frontier: Twenty Cities to Watch," Future Capital Research report by Rajesh Shukia and Roopa Purushothaman.

43. Danwei.org, December 13, 2005, citing the Women's Federation of China.

44. Ernst & Young report, "The Rise of Female Consumerism in China," 2007.

45. Huakun Women's Life Investigation Centre, Beijing.

46. Ibid.

47. All-China Women's Federation, "Urban Chinese Say 'I Do' Ever Later, Study Finds," January 4, 2008.

48. Ernst & Young, "The Rise of Female Consumerism in China."

49. "Modern Women Favor Luxuries," Women of China, Data Research, December 10, 2007.

4: Pink Is Not a Strategy

1. A. G. Lafley and Ram Charan, *The Game Changer* (New York: Crown Business, 2008), 47.

2. Ibid.

3. Data from Procter & Gamble's Swiffer website, October 2008.

4. Andrew Adam Newman, "Embracing Women's Inner Goddess," *New York Times,* February 21, 2008.

5. *BusinessWeek* Product Review by Heesun Wee, February 14, 2001.

6. Matthew Rudy, "How Healthy Is Our Game?" *BusinessWeek,* May 26, 2008.

7. Callaway 2008 earnings announcement, released January 27, 2009.

8. Alex Pham, "Nintendo at the Top of Its Game," *Los Angeles Times,* October 27, 2008.

9. Dave Rosenberg, "Wii Fit Sales to Surpass Grand Theft Auto IV," CNET News, October 21, 2008.

10. Pham, "Nintendo at the Top of Its Game."

5: Marketing to Women

1. "Who Gets Paid What," Ad Age Data Center, 2007; author's research; and Spencer Stuart Study of the top 100 consumer CMO's (66%).

2. Daniel G. Amen, *Sex on the Brain* (New York: Three Rivers Press, 2007), 54.

3. Cambridge Women's Pornography Cooperative, *XXX Porn for Women* (San Francisco: Chronicle Books, 2008).

4. "Multi-tasking Media Users Merge Internet with TV, Other Media," Burst Media Research study, October 2007.

5. Going Green, A Yankelovich Monitor Perspective, July 2007;

and 2007 Cone Cause Evolution and Environmental Survey Research Report.

6. "Volunteering in the U.S. 2008," U.S. Bureau of Labor Statistics news release.

7. Marianne J. Legato, *Why Men Never Remember and Women Never Forget* (Emmaus, PA: Rodale Press, 2005), 139.

8. Deborah Tannen, *You Just Don't Understand* (New York: Quill, 1991).

9. BlogHer/Compass Partners 2008 Social Media Study.

10. "Women and the Web: How Women Are Shaping the Internet," research report by comScore, June 2010.

11. "Online, Women More Likely to Trust Each Other," by Jenna Goudreau, Forbes.com, January 20, 2011.

12. "What Men and Women Are Doing on Facebook," by Jenna Goudreau, Forbes.com, April 26, 2010.

13. comScore, Inc. study, "Women on the Web: How Women Are Shaping the Internet," 2010.

14. Yankelovich Y*Report, "Consumers in Control: Customer Service in the Age of Consumer Empowerment," 2007.

15. Ibid.

16. Ibid.

17. Southwest Airlines data, based on U.S. Department of Transportation Air Travel Consumer Reports from 1987–2009.

6: THE LAST THREE FEET

1. CNW Research, 2008.

2. J. D. Power & Associates, 2008.

3. American Girl website and Chicago Public Library Foundation Newsletter, vol. 5, Fall/Winter 2008.

4. Aili McConnon, "Lululemon's Next Workout," *BusinessWeek,* June 9, 2008.

5. Media Metrix Worldwide Data cited in the comScore Inc. study, "Women on the Web: How Women Are Shaping the Internet," 2010.

6. comScore 2010 Digital Year in Review report.

7. Pew Internet and American Life Project, online shopping report, February 13, 2008.

8. "Online Shopping Needs Improvement," Opinion Research Corporation survey, April 21, 2008, as cited on emarketer.com.

9. Ibid.

10. "Gender, Design, and Marketing," Gloria Moss, 2009, Gower Publishing Ltd.

11. Michael J. De La Merced, "Comcast Buying a Publisher of Net Newsletters and Sites," *New York Times,* August 6, 2008.

ACKNOWLEDGMENTS

I've been on the receiving end of so much kindness and generosity in the process of writing this book.

First and foremost, I stand on the shoulders of incredible pioneers in the fields of linguistics, marketing, and science. The peerless Deborah Tannen's work in identifying gender as cross-cultural communication has profoundly impacted both my work and this book. Maria Bailey's drive to teach the world the power of the "mom" market has been an inspiration, and I am grateful to count her as a friend. Marti Barletta's trailblazing work in applying the concept of gender culture to business has been important and influential, and the field of marketing is all the richer for it.

The work of Daniel G. Amen, M.D., Louann Brizendine, M.D., and Marianne J. Legato, M.D., FACP, has contributed greatly to my own—and the world's—understanding of brain differences between the genders. Many thanks to Mark Osadjan, Ph.D., of the University of Chicago, who possesses a talent for explaining complex science to laypeople.

My agent, Jennifer Joel of ICM, saw the potential for this book from the very first, and it would have never existed without her wisdom and support. My thanks to Jenn, and to the delightful Niki Castle.

I've had the great fortune to work with editor John Mahaney at Crown Business, whose guidance, talent, and dry wit brought out the best in me, and made this book better than I could have imagined. I am eternally grateful. Jo Rodgers, thank you for your constant enthusiasm and understanding.

My good friend, the talented journalist Jeff Bailey, helped guide me through the early and awkward attempts at expressing my thoughts, and taught me how to think like a writer.

Joe Versace selflessly opened every door he could for me in New York and has been a true friend since the day we met. Samantha Ettus made the introduction that made this book possible, and I will always be grateful.

Anne Marie Carver leveraged her charm, intellect, and project management skills to organize the many tasks involved in making this book come together. Her wisdom helped me untangle my thoughts on a daily basis. Rich Carver graciously contributed his graphic design skills.

Lauren Zeinfeld worked with me as an intern while she was still an undergraduate and proved herself to be a prodigy. Fearless and bright, she is a star in the making, and one day I will brag to people "I knew her when."

Kristie Rowling took me across the finish line with this book as a research maven extraordinaire, helping me with the arduous task of fact-checking the final proofs.

Eric Elder of Ryland Homes has been a staunch supporter of this book since day one, and I feel fortunate to call him both a client and a friend. Rob Matteucci of Evenflo has given me more than my fair share of his time and wisdom, and he never fails to make me see the world in new ways.

In India, Roopa Purushothaman and Shefalee Vasudev

helped to enlighten me about the country's complex culture and its magnificent women.

In China, Kunal Sinha and Adam Schokora helped guide me through the complexities of that fascinating country.

To all the executives, medical experts, and women who generously shared their stories and insights for this book, my heartfelt thanks.

I owe a debt of gratitude to Dan Edelman, who always believed in me and gave me the courage to stretch myself in ways I never thought I could. Jerry Epstein enabled my dreams for a female-focused business to take root at Zeno, and I will always be grateful his support, friendship, and zeal for life.

My wonderful gang of friends in Chicago (you know who you are) has been with me every step of the way, celebrating victories large and small, and cheering me on. Susanna Negovan's creative brainstorming has been invaluable.

My mother, Rosemarie Brennan, has instilled in me a lifelong enthusiasm for learning new things, seeing new places, and meeting new people. These qualities have served me well in writing this book. Whatever success I've had in life, I owe to her. Thank you, Mom.

My sisters, Katy, Mary Ellen, Patricia, and Caroline, are four of the biggest reasons I've always found female culture so fascinating. Thank you for being my best friends and unending sources of inspiration.

My wonderful in-laws, Bob and Bibi Orelind, and the entire Orelind and Lamy families of California, have adopted me as one of their own. Their unflagging love and support have enriched my life a thousandfold. Joe Smith has listened to all my book stories with the patience of a saint.

My husband, Erik Orelind, is the person I admire most in the world. Brilliant, hilarious, and kind, he inspires me to be a better person and has always been my greatest source of support. He makes our marriage the most delightful study of gender differences I could possibly imagine.

Index

About the Author

As the oldest of five sisters, it was only natural that **BRIDGET BRENNAN** developed an interest in the needs and wants of women. She is the founder and CEO of Female Factor, a strategic consultancy that advises companies on how to increase their success with women consumers.

Brennan developed her craft as an award-winning agency executive, working with major clients such as Whirlpool Corporation, Johnson & Johnson, Evenflo, Ryland Homes, Pizza Hut, Colgate-Palmolive, United Airlines, and Sprint, among others. She was named U.S. Public Relations Agency Practitioner of the Year by *PRNews* for her work in applying gender psychology to communications.

Brennan has served as an instructor at Northwestern University's graduate program in marketing communications at Medill, and a guest lecturer at the Kellogg School of Management. She is a founder of the Marketing to Moms Coalition and an active member of the Network of Executive Women and the National Speakers Association. She lives in Chicago.

More information about Brennan can be found at www.thefemalefactor.com.